OUR LIFE BEYC _ _____ __

AN INCREDIBLE JOURNEY

A medium's observations and conclusions

(Revised January 2021)

Leanne Halyburton

How The 'Dead' Connect With Us - And

Vice Versa

Daniel Beyond Death

Contemporary

You Wear It Well

If He's Jerking You Around, Dump Him
- He Isn't Mr Right!

Table of Contents

Quick intro!

The last thing you might expect an experienced medium to talk about is scepticism. But I *have* been sceptical, and I *have* questioned, and I *have* challenged - myself, mostly.

You see, it is so easy to become caught up in the drama, and to end up repeating and teaching the same stuff that someone else has repeated and taught to us - without ever asking ourselves if it actually makes *sense* to us? Over the years I came to intensely dislike the way in which spiritual communication was being presented through the media, recognising that huge pressure was being exerted upon popular 'celebrity' mediums by those who wanted to make lucrative television programs and sell lots of books. I have no problem with money being made; we live in a commercial world and the ridiculous days of expecting intuitive individuals to give their skills away for nothing have long gone (I hope).

However, things became stretched and distorted, and the 'real' message was lost - the message about how life and death fit together, and how amazing that process is; the message that reminds us that the physical life that is lived *before* death is a powerful, vital link in the chain of each soul's individual existence - and that nothing is ever lost or deemed meaningless. The focus became the medium him or herself and how 'good' they were (and some *were* and *are* incredibly good at what they do); but it all became a bit of a galloping roadshow in which people's emotions were being manipulated and played upon in order to attract viewings. Over time, I experienced less and less desire to be a part of that, even though I gave hundreds of stage demonstrations and featured on radio. Nowadays, only a very tiny part of my business is dedicated to mediumship, but my belief in the ongoing sense of *self*, and in a continued awareness, has strengthened and grown. We are all going to die from this world one day. I don't shun the idea, dismissing it as morbid or scary, although I am in no hurry to go! And, of course, I especially don't want my loved ones to go because I would miss them with every ounce of my being - at least until I pop my own clogs. I don't spend my life wondering what to expect when I die, but I *do* feel that it is a subject we should all explore - one that we *should* question and challenge. I am not asking anyone to believe exactly what I believe, or to view the journey of life *after* life in the same way that

I do; my truth is just that: mine. It might not be yours. I have a feeling that our experience beyond physical death is personal and unique to each soul... a bit like DNA. My only intention with this book is to share: stories, perceptions, and possibilities. Even if you disagree with some or all of my ramblings, I hope you will find something that makes you smile and even raises a question or two; after all, there should always be room for an extra little bit of food for thought!

Chapter 1

A little bit of backstory!

The young man placed a bottle of red wine on the table and stepped back, smiling. I had no idea who he was but my customer recognised the description - and she understood his message completely. "He was a good friend and would often bring me a bottle of my favourite Merlot," she explained.

The young girl watched me from the corner of my kitchen. She was wearing a light coloured hoodie and chewing on her thumb, which was poking through a hole in the cuff. She 'communicated', through images in my mind, that whilst dressing her for her coffin they had struggled to put one of her shoes on. Her mother, listening to me at the other end of the telephone line, knew nothing about it. Several days later she emailed me to say that she had been in touch with the funeral home, and yes, they'd confirmed that they *had* had problems fitting one of her daughter's shoes.

The little boy showed me an image of himself walking through a doorway and I understood that he had passed very suddenly indeed: here one moment, gone the next. I was told that he'd suffered a sudden, fatal, heart failure. He kept showing me a toy vehicle whilst making "brmm brmm" noises, over and over again. My customer, his mother's friend, had attended the funeral and she explained that it was probably his favourite Ghostbusters car which had been placed on top of his coffin.

The little girl, who'd passed only hours earlier, 'showed' me the rocking horse that had been on her hospital ward... and how she would hold her nose because of the smell of her father's breath. I was a little uncomfortable delivering *that* particular message but her mother laughed, explaining that her husband loved to eat cheese and onion crisps and her daughter always hated the smell! The child also communicated that a tree was being planted in her honour, but her mother was baffled; they were still coming to terms with the loss of their daughter and hadn't thought that far ahead. The following day a friend called to let them know that they had planted a tree in her memory.

These days I no longer do much as a medium, for a number of reasons (none of them sinister!). Sadly, as the years have passed by, I have forgotten many of the stories told by those who are no longer physically with us. But, the sense of being part of something greater than anything I can see with my eyes or feel with my conscious senses has grown stronger and stronger. I used to worry, to seriously question *everything*, even whilst working as a medium. I was uncomfortable with the twee, neatly packaged version of life after death that was often presented and accepted as absolute fact; so much of it didn't make any sense to me. I desperately wanted to understand what it was all *really* about and to deliver an authentic service to my customers. I wanted them to be able to really feel the essence of their loved ones and not just provide them with dry bits of 'evidence'. I often felt inadequate, fearing that even the best I was able to deliver wasn't good enough - and that no matter what I *was* able to receive and explain, I always believed it should be more!

However, I did begin to realise that very often it is the small, seemingly inconsequential things that mean so much to the grieving customer: a bottle of red wine; a shoe that wouldn't fit; a toy car; a little family joke. I have heard many people sneeringly ask, "if we can communicate with the dead, how come they never tell us anything important or earth-shattering?"

Well, I don't think it's their job to do so. And who would believe it if old Auntie Minnie, who'd lived and died in the same small village, going nowhere and doing nothing out of the ordinary throughout her entire life, suddenly started spouting politics or great mystical truths through some random medium? Inspiration and wisdom have always been available to the living from within ourselves, *and* from outside sources. It isn't up to our deceased relatives and friends to proffer mind-blowing enlightenment; it is up to us, whilst here in the physical world, to seek it out for ourselves.

Having said that, souls *do* occasionally come out with interesting little nuggets of information that prove to be unnervingly true! I remember one consultation in which the customer's mother communicated that two people were going to lose their lives on the road, locally, and very soon. I was surprised by the message, to say the very least, as was the woman's daughter. I seriously questioned myself, wondering if, for some weird reason, I had just cooked that one up in my head. However, the consultation took place on a Tuesday - and on the following Friday, whilst driving the children to school, we found that the road had been closed by the police. Two young men, travelling to work by car, had been involved in an accident - and sadly, both were killed. I remember thinking, "oh my God, she was right", and feeling shaken to the core. Okay, you could argue that it was just a huge coincidence, but bear in mind that I live in a rural area and not a town or a city in which accidents occur daily. And, some might even suggest that such a prediction was the work of the 'dark side', but I wouldn't agree.

I don't know why that particular lady delivered the message; she had no connection (that I know of) to either of the young men. However, I understood what was being expressed: that things happen *before* they happen - if you see what I mean. The fact that the two young men were going to be in a certain place at a certain time, and take certain actions that would lead to a certain outcome, was already in motion... every last second of it. Yes, an extremely terrifying thought - but also incredibly mind-blowing! It shows that there *is* a much bigger picture at play here than we mortal souls tend to consider, under 'normal' circumstances. Of course, it is very possible that at any point leading up to the accident one or both of them could have made a last-minute change of plan, leading to a different outcome... but it was obviously 'known' that unfortunately that wasn't going to be the case.

It is our own personal belief about death, and life after death, that will influence our overall response to this story. Of course, first and foremost, we are going to feel incredibly sorry for the families of the two boys; after all, it is they who are left behind, they who will miss their beloved one every day of their lives. If we believe that death is wrong, is a dark and lonely place, and that God should only take the bad ones, then we will view all of this with fear and loathing... denial, even. If, however, we genuinely believe that physical life is one tiny but meaningful link in a possibly endless chain, and part of something *much* greater than our current existence, we will still feel sad - fearful even - but not defeated or helpless. We will still miss our deceased loved ones with every ounce of our being until it is our own time to go, but we will know for sure that love, being the most powerful force of all, doesn't just dissipate and disappear like smoke up a chimney. *They* may have finished experiencing this particular part of their existence but *we* haven't - yet. The tough part is not the dying; it is the remaining *until.* That's the bit that requires the most courage - that's the real challenge. And so, when customers would come to me seeking reassurance that the one who had died was 'alright', I would often say, "well, they're fine... but the big question is, what about *you*?"

Quickly going back to the story, over the following two years one of the young men (whose name begins with the letter M) showed up in several different consultations and I got to know him quite well! He had a nice way about him and was popular. He communicated that his parents had become very bitter, telling his friend's parents that they blamed *their son* for the loss of their own, even though he too had died. No-one could judge them, of course, and no-one would ever want to be in their shoes. Some people cope with grief better than others and that's all that can be said.

So, do all of the little stories I have just recounted here prove or explain anything about what happens to us beyond our physical death? No, not really. But they suggest that conscious awareness continues to exist even after the brain and the body has ceased to function. And, that basic communication between what could be called different dimensions of existence *is* possible, through the means of thoughts, feelings, and sensations. I never doubted any of that when I was working as a medium but I desperately wanted to see more of the bigger picture! Accepting that conscious awareness doesn't die with the body is only the tiniest tip of an immeasurable iceberg - and it wasn't enough for me. What *are* we aware of when we pass from this world? What do we *become*? What do we *do*? And do we actually continue to progress, and if so, *how*? These, and other questions, endlessly bounced around inside my head, pushing me to seek greater understanding. It made no sense to me that, following the amazing, strenuous, sometimes arduous, uncompromising, steep learning curve of life on Earth, the end result was an eternity of floating around in the sky with my also deceased relatives, looking down on the living, sending our love and telling them how happy and at peace we are with our new existence. I decided that if that is ALL there is, I'm not going - end of. In comparison, oblivion seemed attractive - at least I'd get a good long sleep!

However, something within me just knew for sure that that *wasn't* all there is, and even though there are billions of questions I will never have answers to, I believe that I *have* managed to put maybe one or two teeny-weeny jigsaw pieces into place (in a puzzle that has more parts than could ever be counted). Each of us may have our own puzzle that is unique and individual to us. We certainly all have our own beliefs, views, and opinions, especially where the subject of life after death is concerned. I have noticed, for example, whilst reading other writers' Amazon book reviews, that some people become incredibly upset when God is mentioned, others are offended because God or religion *isn't* mentioned, and some state that they already know *exactly* what happens beyond death and that the author is wrong. And, I myself came to learn that not everyone actually *wants* to question, or be exposed to other people's questioning; it bothers and unsettles them. And they are, of course, at liberty to feel that way.

One such occasion took place in a large town hall which was hosting an evening of mediumship. Over the years I have performed on stage many, many times, before deciding that it was something I no longer wanted to do. My friend and I saw this event being advertised and we decided to go along. I was becoming a bit jaded and I think that I was hoping that I would feel refreshed... maybe learn something I didn't know, or even pick up a tip or two.

We were the first to arrive, equipped ourselves with a G & T from the bar, and settled down to enjoy the evening. Thirty minutes in I realised that I was paying more attention to the audience of around 120 people than I was to the lady on stage. I was fascinated by their facial expressions and body language. Some appeared to be entranced, whilst others were yawning and fidgeting. It was enlightening to experience the process from the hall rather than from the stage!

I suddenly became aware that the medium was explaining to us that when children die, they grow up in 'spirit'. I noticed that some people were keenly nodding in agreement. She then asked if anyone had any questions; I did, and I raised my hand.

"Do you believe in reincarnation?"

She smiled and responded with an emphatic, "Yes, I do!"

I had another question.

"And you also believe that children continue to grow up after they die?"

Again she was emphatic. "Absolutely!"

Hmm... okay, *now* I had to ask *another* question.

"Could you explain how the two beliefs are compatible with one another? If you believe in reincarnation then you believe that the soul is experienced and not *new*; it is the *body* that is new, enabling that soul to *revisit* the physical dimension. Because of death the new body is no longer functioning and the revisit is concluded. If the soul *is* an old, experienced one, then what age or stage does it actually grow up *to*?"

She went around the houses, not really answering, and when I said that I didn't understand what she was saying she snapped, "I'm only repeating what I've been taught!". Some members of the audience were glaring at me, willing me to shut my big mouth - which I did. After all, they too had paid to see this lady and they weren't appreciative of someone creating distractions. I understood.

I genuinely wasn't attempting to undermine the medium but I really wanted to hear her explanation. She'd asked for questions and I had put mine to her. I was initially baffled by the irritation of those around me until it clicked with me: they were *comfortable* with their beliefs about children and death, and they didn't want those beliefs to be challenged. I almost wished that I had kept my questions to myself. I didn't want to go around upsetting others... but that evening reminded me that neither did I want to continue working in a way that didn't feel right to *me*. Maybe the medium went home that night asking bigger questions of herself; maybe some of the audience members did the same. Maybe none of them did. Questions can open up doors that can lead to and open up even bigger doors (to the *unknown*, gulp!); sometimes we just want to keep those doors not only firmly closed and locked, but boarded up too!

Now, you might ask why I can't just leave well alone? Why don't I settle on a set of beliefs and have done with it? Or, just walk away from the whole bloody subject and forget about it? Well, because one day *I* am going to die... and because I am completely sure that my life before and after death are inextricably linked - that one naturally follows on from the other as part of an ongoing process. Some will say, "oh, I'm not going to waste my time worrying about what happens after I pop my clogs... I have to live for today."

Well, I'm *not* worrying. But, having peeked through the tiniest of gaps in the door to the 'afterlife', I am stuck with it; that door can no longer be closed. Having seen deceased people I have never met and didn't even know existed, giving snippets of meaningful information to living people I have only *just* met or spoken to, requires further consideration. It is *important*.

Chapter 2

Sweet release and the power of life force!

Our beloved old dog, Sue, was incredibly poorly. That morning, she'd fainted, and I watched, horrified, as she appeared to pass out before tumbling down the three steps into the kitchen, biting her lip in the process. She came to, looking confused and disoriented. But still, I truly believed that following veterinary treatment we would be bringing her home. I was wrong; she had less than a quarter of her kidney function and there was no hope. I was holding her in my arms as the vet injected her and my partner had his arms around me. Suddenly, the most wonderful, amazing sensation of peace flooded through me… and it wasn't just emotional, it was physical too. "Has she gone?" I asked, and the vet confirmed that yes - our faithful, funny, brave little terrier had left this world behind, and of course we sobbed (I am weeping as I type this!).

But, what I experienced as I held her in my arms whilst she moved on blew me away, and I will never, ever forget it. She'd been iller than we understood, and she was weary. Clearly, physical 'death' released her in the most liberating way. I know that some will say that that was just my own imagination, my own feelings, but I really don't care. I didn't *expect* that experience... it took me by complete surprise. To this day I feel honoured to have been able to share it with her. *We* still grieved. Our cats were unsettled for days, whilst the remaining dog, looking unhappy and confused, returned to sniff around Sue's resting place in the garden again and again. She went into a bit of a decline over the following 6 months, becoming clingy in a way that she'd never been. But that was about the living, wasn't it? That was *us*, missing Sue; unfortunately, where there is love, there is always the possibility of loss, though none of us would ever sacrifice the one in order to avoid the other (see how brave love causes us to be?). But, every time I dust the picture of Sue that sits on the shelf below the television, I kiss it, and remember how I felt when she slipped out of this world... and I can just *feel* her life force, her funny little characteristics. She is more alive than ever... just not *here*, in this physical world.

Niki Lauda, three times Formula 1 world champion, explained in a television interview that, following the horrific racing accident in which he was severely burned, he felt as if he was slipping away… and starting to feel comfortable (I am paraphrasing here, as I can't remember exactly how he expressed it), so he consciously *pulled* himself back. He wanted to live, to compete. But that meant facing ongoing agony and permanent scarring. I truly admire and respect Niki Lauda for many reasons, one being that, *six weeks* after being involved in a crash that almost killed him, *and* despite being petrified, he was back in a racing car - finishing fourth. There is something about the human spirit and will that is absolutely life-affirming and encouraging. It says "you CAN do more than you believe is possible"... and *that* is something that definitely survives physical death - a force that cannot be diminished or snuffed out. (Since I wrote this, very sadly indeed, Niki Lauda passed from this world. My partner and I were both heartbroken, feeling a huge sense of loss, even though we had never been lucky enough to meet him. One night, soon after his death, I had a dream in which he told me to be 'resilient'; a couple of days later I watched an interview in which Mercedes team principal, Toto Wolff, was asked to describe the Niki that he knew and loved. One of the very first things he said about him was that he was resilient. I was blown away - surely, that was no random coincidence? And even if others argue that it was, I don't care - I will hold it to my heart forever, and try my best to *be* it!).

I have read many reports from individuals who, whilst on the brink of death, have experienced a sudden and strong sense of ease and relief, before 'returning' to life. One was a young man who'd drowned, but was quickly resuscitated by his rescuers; another was a young woman who had been cruelly strangled to the point of unconsciousness. And I recently listened to a thought-provoking interview on the radio, in which a female broadcaster talked about the terrifying and unexpected health problem she had endured the previous year. One day, whilst working, she suffered a brain bleed and collapsed - leaving her in a coma for seventeen days. When she awoke, she was unable to move or talk. Thankfully, with courage and determination, she relearnt how to do both. However, there was one more thing. Before coming out of the coma, she was aware of being given a choice: stay, and face the challenges of recovery, or take the easier option and leave it all behind. In other words, live or die. She chose life.

And I once worked with a lady who, when in her teens, was hit by a car which threw her into the pathway of a second car. Amongst a list of very serious injuries was a shattered pelvis which left her with a permanent limp. However, following the accident she believed that she had been standing up in the street, observing the scene, and fully aware of everything that was going on... until she woke up in hospital, where she was assured that she couldn't possibly have been on her feet and hadn't been conscious when the ambulance arrived. She described her experience as one of calm, curious detachment rather than as a sense of peace, and in her mind, there was no question at all that it happened that way. Since then, I have come across a variety of near-death stories and my conclusion is that there *are* people out there who have hovered between life and death and have lived to tell the tale. There will be different reasons for this, I imagine, unique to the individual, but one thing is for sure: without their testimonies, we wouldn't know that physical death does not mean instant and complete oblivion - that we *do* actually continue with awareness.

Of course, their accounts will not be accepted by everyone. Some will dismiss them as pure fabrication; others will claim that what they experienced was nothing more than an illusion created by a distressed brain. One or both might be right, one or both might be wrong; however, I feel more inclined to listen to my own intuitive reasoning and those who *know*, through experience, what it feels like to be on the brink of leaving their physical life behind. However, whilst writing about the above stories, it occurred to me that if we had no fear of death, the world would be a very different place. It is never going to be that way, of course, because our dread of death is really the dread of separation. A lot of people will say that they don't fear their own death but do fear the loss of loved ones. Secondary to the dread of separation is anxiety about the unknown. It is probable that the main reason we human souls seek out information about life after death is reassurance; we need to have it confirmed that our deceased family, friends, and pets are not eternally lost to us. We also want to be sure that we ourselves are not facing oblivion, because that would make the life we have lived seem meaningless. And, of course, there is the completely understandable fear of the nature of our death; we would all prefer to slip peacefully away in our sleep!

But, what if we *did* have no fear of dying? Other human beings would cease to have power or control over us. We could no longer be coerced into anything under the threat of death - the ultimate choice of weapon for those who seek to cruelly dominate us. It's a strange conversation to be having, I know; nevertheless, I couldn't help but wonder how life on Earth would be if we were completely free of that fear? I suspect that the reason the near-death experience exists is so that we can be afforded a glimpse into the next part of the journey, with the intention being to inform and reassure us. And we human souls will continue to be inspired by those who face their own death with dignity and courage - the souls who have made peace with the experience that lies ahead of them.

Up to this point in my life, I have only seen two deceased people, but in both cases I was deeply struck by how 'empty' they appeared to be… as if they'd just packed up and gone, leaving their bodies behind. And, although it isn't exactly the same, two years ago I awoke, bleary-eyed, in the early hours of the morning, to briefly 'see' my friend's mother standing beside the bed, smiling. I knew that this lady had recently been taken into hospital for tests and was due out the following day. I reached for my phone, intending to text my friend, but then thought better of it; after all, what the hell was I going to say to her? "Hi, sorry for disturbing you at 2 a.m. but I thought you might like to know that your mum just showed up in my bedroom"?

I went back to sleep, telling myself that I had been dreaming, or more likely imagining things; however, when I awoke at 7 a.m. there was a text message waiting for me: "Mum passed away in the early hours of the morning". I was sad but also hugely reassured, not to mention honoured, by the visit. Her death was unexpected; she had developed a health issue that was under investigation, but there was no question that she'd be coming out of hospital. My friend was looking forward to taking care of her beloved mum for a few days until she was ready to return to her own home - and so you can see that it wasn't as if we were just waiting around, anticipating 'the call'. This made the experience all the more real to me, and I will never cease to remember it with gratitude. And although I *saw* her, it wasn't her physical self that I was seeing… it was her *life force*, presented in a shape and form that would be easily identifiable to me. More than twenty years have passed since I first began working as a medium, but I remain as awestruck as ever by the way in which spiritual communication works, be it a mere wisp of a link, or something more mindblowing!

I have come to believe that each of us is a soul, an individual shard of the great creative force of life (which *might* be the same as God, or the Universe, depending upon your beliefs), and that the purpose of our existence is to create! And, if you think about it, that is exactly what we do, whether or not we recognise it: *we create*. A cup of tea, a meal, a home, a family; a business, a work of art, a piece of engineering/technology/architecture; a cure, a solution, a peace process; an argument, a problem, a mess, a war... *all* our own work. And some of what we create will leave a definite imprint, a testimony to our existence in the physical world, be it on a handful of souls, or maybe even billions. But, in order *to* create inspirationally, a soul in human form has two jobs to do: 1) recognise and learn how to handle ego; 2) embrace and develop spirit. And whilst it is a collaboration between the two that contributes to and shapes our life force, it is the spirit that really needs to have the upper hand! You might ask what any of this has to do with life beyond physical death - and I would explain that it is my own personal belief that when we die, the only thing we take with us is the nature and the dynamic of our spirit. And I believe that we, the individual soul, absorb all that our spirit has become throughout our physical incarnation... and that an imprint is *also* made upon the collective soul (the energy field of *everything* that exists), so that nothing is ever insignificant, or forgotten, or lost... ever!

The life force is the *essence* of the soul we have known and loved, and it is that that we miss the most. However, it is also the life force that continues the journey, and the life force that can sometimes be intuitively felt and seen by those still passing through the physical world. It is energy set free, to continue to grow and develop and to thrive. Life force cannot die, and the 'end' of life, as we call it, is actually the beginning of a different

29

aspect of life... with each soul ultimately deciding upon the nature of his or her own evolution!

Think about the elderly relative whose body was frail and weak... but whose weary eyes displayed a determined, inextinguishable sparkle, right up until they closed for the very last time.

Think about the young person who, understanding that their time on earth was coming to a premature end, reached out to inspire others, endeavouring to make a difference before they left.

Think about the baby, the tiny child, completely innocent and untouched by society's inevitable programming. How pure and sweet was the life force, the essence which touched, and remained with, all who associated with them.

Think about the adventurers, the chancers, the boundary-pushers, the competitors... how can the vibrancy of those souls just fizzle out and cease to exist?

Remember the Stephen Hawkings of this world... powerhouses of curiosity, intelligence, and humour, despite being encased in increasingly painful and unresponsive bodies.

Remind yourself of all that has been left behind for the human race to enjoy, appreciate, and *use*, long after the creators have moved on from this world. Music, literature, paintings, and sculptures; architecture, roads, bridges, furniture, machines, fashion - the list is endless. And every last one started as a thought, an idea, in the mind of a vibrant soul, who then took the kind of action that transformed their vision into a physical reality. Life force in motion, and at its absolute best!

But, what about those poor souls whose experience of life on earth was so challenging that short-term survival was all they could possibly hope for? Or, those who left the world in a horribly cruel way? Or, who endlessly struggled with deepest, darkest depression? Am I saying that *these* souls are without life force? Absolutely not: life force is as much about emotion, courage, strength, and the ability to face the harshest of challenges, as it is about creativity, enthusiasm, and joy. Those who have suffered have provided the most important legacy of all: the opportunity for the human race to consistently recognise and understand the need for tolerance, acceptance, kindness, empathy... and love. And I have *seen* souls who have entered into a form of healing, beyond their physical death. The consciousness can be as traumatised as the body, maybe even more so, but each soul's experience will be unique to them, as will be the healing. I remember, many years ago, seeing a young man who had ended his own life. He was seated in what appeared to be a hardback chair, looking glum, elbow on his knee, chin in his hand... and he was surrounded by brilliantly shining, outstretched arms, patiently waiting for him to become ready to accept their help. He was most definitely not alone. And there have been many others who have shown themselves seated in plump, comfy chairs, catching their breath so to speak... some of whom have even been holding a cup of tea, even though, when we are physically deceased, we don't have lungs to breathe, or a stomach to digest food and drink! It seems to me that we can continue to experience some of the things that have been comfortingly familiar to us - possibly until we no longer need them.

A physical incarnation *is* a big deal. We enter into this world as vulnerable, dependent beings, completely reliant upon those who got here before we did. As we grow, every single day will bring challenges and choices - and the most important choice we will ever make is how we are going to perceive this life we find ourselves in, *and* the world around us. Some automatically slip into the general flow, rarely questioning or challenging anything they are presented with, absorbing it as their *own* truth and reality; some question, but only to a certain point; others scrutinise life, refusing to accept anything at face value, relentlessly seeking a greater and deeper understanding. It doesn't matter which category we fall into... life on earth is still a full-time job. Energetically, we *all* fill the space we occupy with who we are being - it is just that some seem to have more elastic sides than others. Getting through everyday life, processing all of the emotions we will experience, facing our fears, doubts, hopes, and dreams, whilst living amongst billions of other souls who are *also* trying to figure out their own pathway, is going to leave its mark on us, from the inside out.

Then, there is the loving of others and of life itself, which is the most rewarding but risky thing of all. The moment we allow ourselves to love, the risk of loss or rejection rises like mercury in a thermometer on the hottest day of the year - yet thankfully, despite those risks, we seem incapable of giving up on it!

Chapter 3

What do we do?

When I think about what potentially lies beyond this life experience, I feel excited and uplifted! I believe that those creative, adventurous souls who took our collective breath away, with their talent, passion, and courage, continue to energetically feed this physical dimension. When I need real guidance, or inspiration, I open my mind to those I have never met, but love and admire anyway. And I am humble, asking for rather than demanding a connection - whilst apologising for mithering! It is usually wisdom, inspiration, or general guidance that I feel most in need of, when reaching out to my spiritual 'heroes'. I just know that they are as passionate and as driven as they were whilst exploring this physical world - and I am sure that they remain true to who they are, in the great life beyond. After all, that kind of energy is inextinguishable! I see them seeking out their own heroes, and looking for solutions to those frustrating, unsolvable problems they battled with when alive. And the souls who come into this world appearing to be completely naturally talented are souls who have brought that with them. As have the souls whose determination leaves the rest of us in the shade, or whose bravery has us on the edge of our seats. They might not always be the most easy-going individuals, or the most saintly; after all, they *are* experiencing themselves in physical form, and no-one is perfect! There are even animals who are clearly different - animals who appear to be almost human, somehow. We have had cats who are, well - cats. But we had one in particular who behaved in ways that made us wonder if she'd somehow gotten into the wrong body! And now we have one who appears, to all intents and purposes, to be a dog. What went on *before* they arrived in this life... that's what I'd like to know!

The question of what souls do, beyond their physical existence, is one that has intrigued me for a very long time. I have agonised over it, desperate not to settle for anything that feels conveniently comfortable. A 'truth' absolutely needs to make sense to us if we can hope to have any faith in it. I understand that we human souls tend to adopt beliefs that allow us to feel comfortable and reassured - and is ideally a complete story, with the t's crossed and the i's dotted. Blurred edges can be a nuisance, often throwing up the kind of questions that lead to doubt. And we don't want to doubt - we want to believe! I have come to a firm conclusion that, when in purely energetic form, each soul chooses its own reality. However, it is important to remember that that is *my* belief, and I am aware that not everyone will agree. But that's exactly the point, isn't it? I don't feel inspired by the version of the 'afterlife' that is accepted as truth by some people; and, in turn, those people are likely to reject *my* proposition. None of us can truthfully swear that we are absolutely correct in our beliefs, can we? However, here's an intriguing thought: what if we are *all* correct?

If we view the concept of life after death through our own filter (which we do), a filter that is coloured by our personal perceptions, then how can a one-size-fits all experience be awaiting us in a life beyond? If you are right and I am wrong - or vice versa - does that mean that one of us will be stuck with an existence that makes no sense to us and causes us to feel lost or displaced? As a child, I attended a staunchly Catholic school, and the message was, "we are right and everyone else is wrong. Unless you adhere to these teachings you aren't going to make it into heaven" - and even then, that kind of approach didn't convince me. If you think about it, here on good old planet Earth, we are playing our role in creating the life that we live through our choices and our actions (although circumstance is definitely more against some than it is others). The life *I* choose to live is not necessarily the life that you choose; your idea of what is desirable and fulfilling is probably not going to match mine. So - why would it be any different when we leave this incarnation behind?

Now, this next part is going to be tricky. I have dillied and dallied over it, consistently finding other things to do rather than write! I was recently discussing my trepidation with my youngest daughter, and she hit the nail squarely on the head: "so, you really want to express your personal truth, but you are concerned about alienating readers?" Bingo, that's it in a nutshell! I want to be able to present my case without upsetting anyone. For example, I don't long to be reunited with many of my deceased relatives, and not because I hate or fear them. I am just detached. I view the souls who were my parents as humans I have known and had some degree of history with, but who are now experiencing themselves in energetic form; not authority figures... just equals. However, that is a reflection of the way in which I experienced them in life. My childhood wasn't easy and I was living alone and paying my own way in the world at the age of 17. I genuinely bear them no ill-will, and would be interested in experiencing them as they are now. I picture my father as a young man in his thirties, not for any reason other than that's how he appears on the screen of my mind whenever I think about him. And the same with my mother; I genuinely feel that she is free to be the non-conformist she always was - but no longer getting into trouble! They are not together, in the accepted sense (it didn't take much for them to enrage each other whilst alive!). Nevertheless, they jointly wrote some history together, before angrily going their separate ways; I feel that now they probably respect that chapter from the story of their mutual journey - but are happy to explore their own individual pathways. I have no wish to spend eternity with them, although I do have love for them. And though I don't have a burning desire to immediately connect with them when I die, I believe that we will still 'feel' the essence of each other. Conversely, there are now-departed souls who inspired me in so many ways that I look forward to expressing my heartfelt love and gratitude toward them. Individuals whose unconditional generosity and kindness pulled me back onto the straight and narrow, over and again - even when I didn't deserve it. There are others, too, I remain inspired by, long after their passing - and whom I look forward to being *further* inspired by! I believe, with all of my heart, that there is much to rise to and explore - if we so wish.

And so, I come back to the suggestion that we choose our own reality when we leave this world behind. We are vibrational beings - physically *and* energetically. Around 99% of our body is made up of atoms, which are composed of particles - and particles are in constant motion (a bit of clumsily expressed science for you). Even though we appear to be solid, apparently we aren't! We all emit vibrational energy, which can't be seen with the human eye but can be felt (more commonly known as the energy field). But, what happens when we die? Our body is either buried or burned. Well, we continue to vibrate, but at a much higher frequency. We are consciousness in motion, and the way we function is very different to the way we do when connected to the physical body. We don't use our hands to create something, we use our imagination. However, we can *picture* ourselves using our hands - and probably find that we are more efficient! And we also picture for ourselves the life after death that resonates with us. If we choose circumstances that strongly mirror the life we have lived, then that is likely to be our experience. For many, that will include permanent connection with loved ones who have gone before. I have heard a lot of human souls describe the afterlife as being pretty much the same as their physical life, only sunnier, and with no worries or problems. And, to be honest, there's probably a lot to be said for that! I know that I spoke about not having a burning desire to reconnect with some souls simply because we were related by blood - but I can't bear the thought of being disconnected from others, such as my children, partner, and pets! And I don't believe that I will be. However, my vision for myself is huge, because I also envisage an endless adventure of exploration and discovery. Imagine a limitless library, containing every experience that has ever been had (or is ever likely to be had), *and* everything that has ever been felt, known, invented, created, discovered, understood, and solved... plus so much more! For the curious soul, that would be actual heaven. That said, I don't believe that every soul automatically has immediate and absolute access to this golden source of knowledge and wonder - I think that probably we can only be aware of that which we are currently able to align with. There is no librarian checking our application forms or date-stamping our cards. We can only be open to that which we are, well... open to. But, I also believe that we can continue to become more enlightened, which in turn grants us greater access to higher levels within what I affectionately call the 'library' (or, as it is often referred to, the Akashic Records).

Of course, this isn't going to be everyone's idea of bliss! It will sound too much like hard work to some, especially if they have had no interest in such things whilst physically alive. The world weary, the exhausted, the sick, and the depressed - their initial dream will doubtless be one of peace, rest, and healing. The lonely and grieving will, first and foremost, look forward to loving reconnection with deceased loved ones or pets. However, those souls can still be open to so much more, beyond their spiritual recuperation - if they choose to be.

I may have made all of this sound too idealistic - too neatly packaged. If I have, then I haven't expressed myself well enough. It's difficult though, isn't it? We're trying to make sense of something that is way beyond our comprehension, as human souls. And I am aware that there are flaws in my theory - or maybe exceptions to the rule. I think that there is probably a light/dark divide, with the dark operating at a lower vibration than the light. A 'dark' soul who is not open to the light imprisons itself, restricting its own progression, and I can't imagine that it would have access to the glorious source of knowledge and creativity. Unless, of course, it chooses to acknowledge its own nature and opens itself up to the light. And even then, it would be an ongoing work in progress.

I have often been asked the questions "who is my loved one with?" and "who is looking after my loved one?" I don't believe that we need to be taken care of when we die, regardless of our age. We imagine a deceased child being taken in and looked after by a grandparent, as would happen in physical life, but I don't believe that is how it is. There is no danger and no need for babysitters. The soul of a human child is no more vulnerable than the soul of a human adult. In fact, the soul of a child is likely to be more open and in less need of healing than one who has spent years and years on planet Earth, dragging its exhausted backside through one tough experience after another! Again, it is all about love. The child-soul will be immersed in love and nurtured in a spiritual way, not only by those souls known to it, but also by the collective soul. My niece died at the age of 13 and I was strongly aware of her presence for a while - and *always* she presented herself as strong, free, and completely in control! I remember a dream I had, maybe two years after she passed, in which I was absolutely overjoyed to discover that she was actually 'alive'... and she responded by rolling her eyes at me as if I was a complete idiot! *Of course* I am alive, she was saying: what did you *think*? It was one of those dreams that seem so real that waking from it is a shock to the system, and I cried buckets when I realised that she wasn't alive in the physical sense after all - that she was still 'dead'. However, I recognised that she was letting me know that she was still around and within reach - *and* that she still had attitude!

Whilst we're on the subject of those who pass whilst still very young, here is a little food for thought. C was a child who died under tragic and confusing circumstances. It was feared that he had taken his own life, but he assured me that that was not the case: it was accidental, and nothing more. As time passed by, I would periodically be asked to communicate with him again, and I noticed that he was changing - that he appeared to be maturing, somehow. Now, I am aware that I have previously given my view on the idea of children growing up in spirit - but this isn't exactly the same thing. Well, I don't *think* that it is, anyway. I have seen many, many souls who were elderly and frail when they passed, first presenting themselves as they were at the time of their death, before presenting a younger, stronger version. I don't believe that it is a case of growing up, or going backward in time; it is probably more to do with experiencing ourselves in a way that allows us to continue to evolve - and also feels *right* to us. I have never experienced a connection with someone who died young and then grew into old age, so maybe each soul chooses its own 'settling' point, whilst continuing to explore its own potential.

Anyway, here's a question I believe is worth asking: what about those who technically have no-one to take care of them? There have been, and will be, billions of souls who don't have anyone waiting in the wings, so to speak: displaced, abandoned children whose parents were also displaced and abandoned, in poverty-stricken parts of the world; the secret babies, conceived under problematic circumstances, whose lives were terminated in the womb; cruelly treated and abandoned animals; animals slaughtered for food, skin, and fur; all wild animals, including insects. Who takes care of *these* souls? The light does. Each one, even the tiniest and seemingly most insignificant, is drawn back to source, enveloped in love. The energy of each one is also recorded by the collective soul, because it is as much a part of the whole as is everyone and everything else that has ever existed. Nothing is deemed meaningless.

There are no geographical locations in a purely energetic dimension. There are no maps. Even my 'library' can only be accessed through the consciousness. And all communication is mind-to-mind. In my novella, Daniel Beyond Death, fifteen year old Daniel was alarmed when he realised that everything he 'thought' was being heard by other souls, as if he was speaking out loud… at least, until he got the hang of it, that is!

Here is a question I have contemplated many times, searching for an answer that satisfies me. The question is: if a soul leaves a partner and/or children behind, how can they be at peace? I know, through my work, that they *are,* but how is that possible? Looking at it through the emotions of a human soul, it seems inconceivable that the deceased wouldn't be grieving as much as the bereaved. On the other hand, do we really want to believe that our lost loved one is lonely, sad, and unhappy? My questioning, and my meditative contemplation, have led me to suspect that we are not as far apart as we might believe ourselves to be. And this is where it all now becomes a bit more 'out there'!

There are certain sayings and phrases, connected to the subject of life after death, that have become very popular - especially within the spiritualist movement. One of those is "the other side", which is the place people go to when they die. I am probably being pedantic, but that implies that there are only two places in which any of us can possibly exist: here, on planet Earth, or there, in the 'spirit world'. *And* that we can only be in one of those places or the other. Well, I believe that there are many, many dimensions of non-physical existence (some scientists say that there isn't only one universe, there is a group of them - a multiverse - which would suggest that there might well be a plethora of physical dimensions, too). I feel that we can be - and are - in more than place at once. Some part of us remains connected to all that is, to the source of our very existence... like a ray of heat and light emitted by the sun. We aren't shipped out lock, stock, and barrel, disconnected from our power source - but we forget that. We come into this physical existence with what I call 'spiritual amnesia'; or, at least, most of us do. Some souls retain a degree of memory, usually involving past incarnations, though I can't explain why that should be. To remind the rest of us that there *is* more than our limited vision and sense allows us to be aware of? I would say that that sounds feasible. Regardless, I doubt that we'd be able to function in this world if we had full spiritual memory; it would absolutely get in our way. However, we are all equipped with something that can help us to continue to feel connected, in our own chosen way: the capacity for faith. Some human souls elect not to have any faith at all; others become blinded by theirs; and many of us have experienced the agony of suddenly doubting our faith, or losing it altogether. Faith is often the thing that keeps us going through the toughest of times - along with hope.

So, a part of us (let's call it the higher self) remains connected to the whole, even though our human self forgets that. And our higher self continues to whisper to us as we manoeuvre our way through our physical incarnation, doing its best to offer insight and guidance. The souls who have moved on from this world are able to communicate with our higher self, even though our earthly self generally doesn't consciously register it - apart from the odd moments of sudden awareness, or in dreams. Those souls also communicate directly with our earthly self through other means, particularly mediumship. And this is why deceased loved ones don't grieve in the same way that we do - because they still have access to us. Well, that's what I have come to believe, anyway, after giving the subject a huge amount of consideration. And of course, time, as we experience it in this world, doesn't exist in a non-physical dimension - and so *possibly* there is no endless sense of waiting. As I said, this explanation might not resonate with everyone, but at least it is out there for consideration!

A couple of years ago, I heard of the passing of a man I had never met, from other people who *had* known him. And it really got to me, causing me to ponder, once again, how a deceased soul is able to make peace with having to leave precious loved ones behind. He was 40 years old when he died, suddenly and unexpectedly; his wife and two young children were devastated, not to mention his parents and friends. He was one of those stars who shine brightly in the world, enigmatic and passionate, a huge inspiration to others - only to burn out way too soon, leaving a gaping hole that could never be filled. Although I didn't know him, I wondered about his current reality and how things were for him - and so I asked if I could maybe make a link with him. I experienced an incredibly strong feeling that he would always be within the reach of his loved ones, that his love would be with them until their own transitions and beyond, and that he had no regrets - he wouldn't change a thing about the life that he had lived. And, through a kind of 'knowingness', I recognised that he understood and accepted it all, in a way that would make no sense to his grieving loved ones... that his premature passing was actually a part of his own unique journey. When I say that I could feel the depth of his love and gratitude for his life and his legacy, I am not just trotting out a platitude. I am describing how he expressed it to me. I know that that wouldn't even begin to touch the pain experienced by those who will miss his physical presence forever; but, hopefully, they will be able to feel his essence and his life force when they really need it the most.

What of his journey now, though? What is he aware of and what is he capable of? This particular soul, a powerhouse of positive intentions, with an innate desire to help and support others, is never going to spend eternity floating around in the sky, looking down on his still-living relatives and friends, smiling sublimely and wishing them all the best! His enthusiasm, his love of life, and his passion for helping others to develop their own skills and talents was not left behind with his body; in his state of pure consciousness he will continue to develop and explore, and to somehow continue to make a difference, because that is how he was and still *is* - and because, more often than not, his spirit was more in control than his ego.

Chapter 4

Love and reconnection

Souls recognise one another, I believe. Certainly, souls who have shared experiences within the physical dimension automatically resonate, but it makes sense to me that *no* soul is a stranger to us, even if we never actually met whilst in the flesh. We sense them and gain an immediate knowingness about them, especially if there is a reason or a desire for us to connect.

There may be souls we absolutely do not wish to feel, see, or be around again - and because we are creating our own experience of life beyond death, we don't have to do any of those things. It might be that we have the capacity to eventually heal sufficiently enough to experience a genuine sense of detachment toward the source of our pain, though I couldn't say for sure. My reasoning is, if we *continue* to harbour resentment, fear, or hatred toward another soul, then surely we aren't becoming free? That that intense emotion will at least partially prevent us from evolving? However, even if that *is* the case, free will still applies and the choice would be ours.

Love is not something that dies with the body or simply ceases to exist. If we have loved a soul who has left this world before us, the energetic 'body' of that soul *and* the energy of the emotion of love continues to not only exist but to flourish. Why would it not? Death is about liberation, evolution, and growth - and if we love, deeply and strongly, we naturally continue to embrace and nurture it beyond our passing.

I don't believe that sexual jealousy exists beyond physical death and therefore if a soul has had more than one spouse there wouldn't be a need to 'choose' between them; it is love, affection, and kindredship that connects. Just because two people are living together and following an established routine whilst alive, it doesn't automatically follow that that will continue in exactly the same way after they have both died. The loving connection will remain, but, as each soul is unique and individual, it can choose to follow its own natural pathway. In my novella, Daniel Beyond Death, the boy discovers that although his beloved grandparents are 'together', they are also being true to the nature of their individual spirits. Brenda continues to be a nurturer, whilst Bill travels and explores - something he felt unable to do during his physical incarnation. Geographical distance doesn't present a problem in a non-physical dimension because it doesn't exist there; and, as communication is conducted mind-to-mind, it is instantaneous - as are expressions of love and affection!

Loneliness does not exist for those who have crossed the finish line between life and death - except for the stubborn souls who refuse to examine (and then accept responsibility for) their incarnation; and even then it is self-imposed, without a need for permanence. There are no divisions imposed by gender, race, religion, or culture - as discovered by Daniel (from my novella), when he grudgingly agrees to attend church with Grandma Brenda, fully expecting a mind-numbing service held in a musty-smelling building filled with old people... only to be *very* pleasantly surprised!

Chapter 5

How does it feel?

T was just short of his 21st birthday when he was killed in a freak motor accident. It was one of those situations in which a few seconds, either way, would have led to a completely different outcome. His mother told me that, following his birth, she held him for the very first time and just 'knew' that she wasn't going to have him forever, a feeling she did her best to push away and ignore. His family bravely went ahead with his 21st birthday party, days after his passing, because they wanted to celebrate his life, and also to know and appreciate him through his friends' eyes. It was a well-attended party, the tears and the laughter flowed, and T's parents came to understand just how many people genuinely liked and cared for their beloved son. There were no airs and graces about him; he laughed a *lot*; he teased others and played tricks on them; he didn't judge others and he didn't look for trouble or conflict. He worked hard and hoped to fall in love with someone who loved him back. There was nothing bad to say about him... he was an all-round nice guy.

The crematorium was packed, with standing room only. I tried to cry... I wanted to cry. So did everyone else. But somehow, it just wouldn't happen. I 'saw' T standing at the end of his coffin, watching on with interest, and I knew that he absolutely did not want tears and that somehow this was being channeled through the mourners. I believe now that he wanted his parents to have as easy a time as possible - they are incredibly kind people and would have felt duty-bound to comfort those who were grieving, putting their own pain to one side. Also, he didn't want anyone to be sad or downhearted... he wanted to laugh and lark around! I have communicated with him a handful of times since then, and have noticed his progression, with interest, something I have also experienced with other 'deceased' souls. I cannot explain it and I cannot tell you exactly what T is currently up to, but I know for sure he is continuing to develop, in his own way.

This morning, thinking about this book, I decided to make what I term a cosmic phone call, and request a link with him. I wanted to ask him a couple of things, and indeed, I quickly be-came aware of his presence... and the first thing I 'heard' in the centre of my mind, was, "My mum's chips are the best!" Okay, not a mind-blowing statement, but typical of T; he loved his food and he actually worked as a chef! I asked him to explain how he felt at the moment of his passing, and I received a sensation akin to floating, like a bubble moving upward through water... peaceful, pleasant and interesting. Unfortunately, we were then interrupted by something of *this* world, and I said I would get back to him! But I actually had my answer - what it felt like to *him* when *he* died - and I am really grateful that he shared it with me!

I remember one elderly lady revealing to me a scene that I understood to be her experience of the transition from physical life to non-physical. I saw the inside of a lovely old church, and I could smell the polished wood of the pews and the beams, marvel at the sun's rays passing through stained glass windows, causing colours to dance across pale, stone walls. The sensation was one of absolute peace and stillness, and I knew that this soul had nurtured a strongly Christian belief and an unwavering faith in her God. No-one on Earth could reasonably argue that she was delusional - this was *her* reality, *her* truth, *her* spiritual relationship with the great, creative force of life. And it emanated from an entirely loving place.

Deceased people have expressed the experience of their passing in different ways. Being lifted, or almost sucked out of the physical body, is fairly common. One lady, who had become very frail prior to her passing, showed me how it had been for her, when she parted company with her body. There appeared to be strands, connected to her head, shoulders, arms, and torso - rather like silky puppet strings - and she was lifted, gradually, until she was upright, on legs that *had* been shaky and weak, but no longer felt that way. A man and a woman appeared, and it was clear that they were waiting for her. She turned, glanced over her shoulder at her still, tired old body - and then stepped forward, leaving this world behind.

Another lady described feeling as though the years were just dropping away during her transition: as she moved from the worn-out form lying on the bed, her legs felt sturdy and strong, her hair became soft and bouncy, her back straightened, and her lungs became clear. But, the fact is, she no longer *had* a body! How could she be feeling this way when the physicality had ceased to operate and function? I can only conclude that the awareness of self continues and that the physical body is NOT all that we have... that, in fact, it is only a representation of the energetic body: a solid, outer manifestation that comes with a sell-by date, ultimately to be recycled! It represents only a temporary version of the original, which itself continues to thrive, develop, and evolve, through an endless supply of experiences. One man, who had passed in his sixties, was keen to express the huge sense of relief he experienced when he realised that, despite being dead and minus a functioning body, he was still aware!

Some souls die young in a particular incarnation, but are actually highly advanced, energetically speaking, at the time of their passing. Some souls are very elderly, years-wise, when they die, but are not as evolved. Physical age alone doesn't guarantee wisdom and spiritual advancement. One soul may have had more actual *experiences* than another, but the way in which those experiences are absorbed, processed, and utilised, is always going to depend upon individual choice. I believe that life before and after death are connected, like links in a precious and unbreakable chain. Who we become in this world goes with us into the next.

Think about the frail, elderly old man who loves motorbikes, and who has, in his time, ridden what are now considered to be classics. He might be affectionately viewed by younger men, who are tearing around on modern machines, as someone stuck in the past... someone who *used* to ride, before life and age caught up with him. An interesting old guy, but past it. However, inside, that soul is still an adventurer, a risk-taker... a pioneer. After all, today is always built upon yesterday, and tomorrow will always be built upon today. Every human being experiences the effect of those who have gone before, in one way or another. Modern bikes exist courtesy of the old machines, which, in their time, were revolutionary. And as that frail old man takes his last physical breath, he - the soul - is released, as he experiences what he *really* is: vibrant, reckless, passionate… handsome, mischievous and proud. He loved his wife, his children, his life - but he wanted to fly with the wind. Time caught up with his body but never with *him*, the soul!

Think about the elderly woman whose physical mobility is now greatly reduced, and who cannot get out and about without some assistance from others. Inside, that soul is the same one who would slip into her favourite dress, stockings, and heels, brush her hair until it shone, apply lipstick and a dab of perfume… and go dancing, *every* Friday and Saturday night! The same one who would sing along to songs on her favourite radio station whilst cooking Sunday lunch, and who would be the first onto the dance floor at family parties. As she disconnects from her now worn-out body, she takes the music and the dance with her, because it is a vital part of *her*, the soul, and it vibrates within her spirit. She feels uplifted and more and more fluid in movement, as the restrictive heaviness falls away.

A few days ago, I read a local newspaper report about a young man who had recently died in a motor accident, and my first thought was one of huge sadness for his family, followed by, "What is he seeing and feeling *now*? What is he aware of? How *is* he?" It was stated that he loved the beach, and the report included a picture of him strolling along the shoreline with his friends, enjoying the sunset... a completely poignant image. And then, today, as I was on my usual daily walk with our old dog, along the beach and around the woods, with my favourite music blasting through my headphones (there is something incredibly majestic and uplifting about the experience of nature, accompanied by a loud soundtrack of rock and blues!), I paused, as I often do, on a little wooden bridge overlooking an overgrown part of the river where the ducks hide out and the dragonflies dance around your head, never settling long enough for you to fully admire them (it is a bit of a sun trap, surrounded by sloping fields of sheep and darting rabbits, and I like to just stand, breathe and absorb, for a few moments).

Suddenly, I became aware of a presence beside me, gazing over the edge of the bridge and into the narrowed river. We were elbow to elbow, and as I turned, I recognised the outline of a young male - the boy from the newspaper report. For a second I was nonplussed until I remembered that I *had* been thinking about him, on and off, for the last couple of days, (which *would* have reached him, energetically speaking), and that I *had* just been walking along the shoreline, something he himself loved to do. Communication between us took the form of just 'knowing' and feeling, an instant exchange of thoughts and images. The first thought was how he used to love jumping into water from a height, and how, as a kid, he would have been dangling over that bridge even though the water below was shallow! And then he raised his hands to his head, and I understood that he was explaining the cause of his death: head and neck injury.

He also expressed that he was kind of just taking a little time to revisit people and locations that were meaningful to him, but was becoming ready to embrace something else... something that he wanted to show me, visually. I saw him walking towards a bright light (yes, a little predictable, I know!), but he himself was becoming lighter and brighter, and, as I watched, he stretched out his hands, staring in wonder as light poured from his fingertips. The feeling that accompanied this beautiful image was one of joy and excitement, and I knew that he was entering into infinite space filled with infinite possibilities! He moved away, toward the left, and I moved right, toward the steps; as I looked over my shoulder, for a final glimpse, he did the same... and then he was gone. And I smiled to myself when I realised that the music was still pouring from my headphones - and that the song that was playing was, 'Don't Fear The Reaper!' (Since originally writing this, our beloved dog became too ill to remain in this world, leaving a gap that can never be filled. Up to now I have not been able to visit the wood and the beach that we enjoyed daily, because it is still too painful to be there without her. Still, I *am* going to try and make it... soon.)

When a soul leaves this physical world, following ongoing trauma or suicide, it might be in need of comfort, and reassurance that it is now safe - which, of course, would be absolutely forthcoming. If all of existence - past, present, and future - was one, shining, multifaceted jewel, then every soul would be an individual shard, a vital part of the whole, and yet unique in its own way. And it is the collective energy of the *light* element of the whole that supports the individual shards. The physically deceased are energetically absorbed back into the fold, so to speak, but without losing the sense of unique self. If our material universe is expanding - as we are told that it is, by those in the know - then so is our energetic universe... and *we* are an intrinsic part of both. The spiritual, creative expansion requires every experience possible, seen and felt through a trillion different perspectives, trillions of times over. If, upon physical death, we lost our awareness of unique self and just melted into an unconscious mass of energy, there could be no growth, only eventual implosion. Spiritually, every shard is welcomed and supported by the strongest, most healed part of the whole - even if a shard *initially resists*.

One of my very first customers was a man whose partner had committed suicide. She had been struggling with depression for some time, and on the fatal day he had taken their two young children for a walk, whilst she slept. Upon their return the children dashed upstairs, eager to show their mother the things they had collected… only to find that she had taken her own life. At first, I was angry with her: how *could* she subject her family to such a devastating experience? I even told her so, if I remember rightly. However, I quickly came to understand that she loved her family with all of her heart and actually believed that they'd be better off without her. She had sunk into such a dark pit of despair that she was unable to see even the slightest glimmer of light; there was no joy, no hope, and nothing to believe in. As she faded from this world there was no celebration or joyous release… but there *was* a huge sense of relief, as if an unbearable, crushing weight had been lifted from her shoulders.

This world is just too tough for some souls, and that's a fact. It is absolutely heartbreaking for those who are left behind to pick up the pieces and sometimes the shock and grief is expressed as anger, albeit temporarily. But, for the soul who is just too weary and overwhelmed to hang on in there, there is no punishment, no recrimination, and no judgement (is my conclusion). Some say that suicide is a cowardly act, but I don't agree and see it as one of hopelessness and desperation. I can absolutely understand why one customer felt that her husband had ducked out of the responsibilities of life, leaving her alone to raise their children *and* deal with all the problems that he himself could no longer face; the burden must have been unbearable. But, I could also recognise that he had come to see himself as a complete failure as a man, worthless, and useless... and again, that his family would be better off without him. The living *and* the newly deceased will, at times, require loving support and healing, and it will always be available to them - even when the initial shock, overwhelm, and raw pain causes them to throw up a wall of resistance. When a soul is ready, the healing process can at least begin.

Chapter 6

Resistant souls

A good friend of mine who is very spiritually minded once counselled a young man who had many, many emotional issues. His father was cruel and controlling and when he died it seemed that the boy's life would automatically become easier and happier.

Sadly, this was not the case. The emotionally battered son was convinced that his deceased father was haunting him, and so his misery continued. I have to admit, I was sceptical, believing that the boy was probably traumatised and in need of psychological help (and I still believe that was true) - but, the more I learned about what was occurring the more I felt that he could possibly be telling the truth. My friend used to 'clear' buildings that contained negative residual energy, and she held a sitting at the home once shared by the abusive father and his son. Her strong conclusion was that the man was indeed hanging onto his son, fearful of reflecting upon the story of his own life and terrified of punishment. She told me that she had worked to connect with the unhappy soul and had persuaded him to 'move on' for his own ultimate healing - leaving his son in peace.

And I remember visiting the home of a customer (let's call her Angela), who told me that there was a presence in the house - and that this presence had actually physically touched her. She explained how she had been lying on the sofa, facing away from the room, when she felt arms wrap around her. She turned, expecting to see her boyfriend - only to find that she was alone. She still felt as though she was being held, and in a panic she pushed the invisible intruder away with such force that she scratched her own stomach with her finger-nails! As she relayed the story, on the screen of my mind developed an image of a man with black hair and blue eyes, who I intuitively understood to have been a seafarer and a drinker... and that he was looking for his mother. I described this to Angela and she immediately clapped a hand over her mouth in shock. It emerged that the woman from whom she rented the house had grown-up children, all with black hair and blue eyes... and that one son, an alcoholic, who had served in the merchant navy, had sadly died. The woman, who now lived abroad, had recently been back in the UK and had visited Angela. I have to admit that I felt incredibly sad for the poor soul; he was embracing a feminine energy in the home that was once his mother's. I advised her to seek out appropriate help, more for his sake than hers, and I believe that she did so. I never really wanted to become involved in 'clearings', although I did so a couple of times, for friends - with apparently positive results. However, I just didn't feel that it was my forte, and I have seen too many embarrassing dramas being acted out in the name of sending lost souls into the 'light'! I am not saying that every individual whose work requires them to aid lost spiritual entities is deluded or at-tention-seeking… far from it (after all, my friend is one of them. She just wasn't available for Angela). However, we have all seen television programs featuring obviously silly and over-the-top people making a song and dance about urging errant souls to be on their way! I believe that it should be low-key and calm, and carried out by those who genuinely understand what they are do-ing.

I can't explain for sure why some souls hang onto the physical dimension following their passing, except to say that there ap-pears to be a strong connection with a less than ideal attitude and set of behaviours whilst still 'alive'. However, it is not black and white, or simple and straightforward; most of us human beings struggle to be the best possible version of ourselves throughout our lives, and some of us are so emotionally injured or traumatised by our experiences that we survive by default - by inflicting our anger and pain onto *others*. There are also people who have *nothing* to give, for whatever reason, and who abdicate responsibility by neglecting and abandoning those who need them the most. That doesn't automatically mean that they are cold-hearted and uncaring; some, maybe, but not all. And, it also doesn't mean that every soul who has lived a troubled life is destined to be 'earthbound' - there is absolutely *no* evidence to suggest that that is the case. In fact, I have made a connection with many whose lives were filled with personal hardship and who struggled to handle things in the best or most reasonable way - but were basically good people who experienced a sense of regretful relief upon passing, and were open to self-reflection and healing. As I have already said, physical life is not easy for every soul to navigate - in fact, it seems to have the capacity to bring out the *worst* in some, making life incredibly difficult for those who cross paths with them. But, the good news is, for those souls who *do* initially refuse to embrace their own transition, they are never truly stuck - they can choose to do so whenever they are ready - even if a bit of persuasion is ultimately required.

But, what about the really stubborn, misguided souls - the ones who inflict deliberate and intentional misery and suffering upon their fellow human beings, before finally exiting this world? This is awkward to write about because it is a highly sensitive subject, and one that is likely to incite major differences of opinion. My own personal belief is that they are not punished by a higher authority for their gross misdemeanors (I don't believe that any soul is) - I believe that they are their own judge, jury, and jailor - *or* liberator, dependent upon their response. Some human beings become powerfully influenced and programmed by others in the most destructive way possible - utterly brainwashed - to carry out acts that they *believe* are justified, in line with whatever noble cause they have been persuaded to fight for. But, upon physical death, they deeply 'feel' the pain and despair of those they have wronged, and recognise their connection with every other soul on the planet, regardless of culture or religion - and they willingly choose to reflect upon the experience that was their physical incarnation. They committed atrocities but, more enlightened, they accept responsibility and begin to reassess the experience of their life - literal soul-searching - which must be an agonisingly intense process.

And then there are the dark, twisted souls who have absolutely no compunction about acting out their distorted, violent beliefs against innocent people, including those whom they are supposed to love. I do not know why such human beings exist; I don't know if they enter life that way, or become it as a result of experience and programming. My current belief is that some souls *are* born with hatred and loathing already present within them, incubating, just waiting for an outlet. Others will seriously disagree, and I couldn't argue with them - after all, I don't know for sure that I am correct in my assumption. But I also believe that the soul who exits physical life with a hateful, angry, vengeful spirit, and who furiously resists the process of reflection upon the life they have just lived, limits *itself* to a grey, joyless, loveless existence. That soul isn't 'sent' there - it isn't a geographic location - it is a self-imposed state of mind that is impossible to move away from without conscious surrender to genuine soul-searching and re-flection. There is absolutely no way of avoiding personal respon-sibility, upon our physical death. There is no one to hoodwink or persuade; no one to bribe or con; no one to plead our case with. Only ourselves to face, and we either take responsibility for our own choices and actions, or we don't; either way, there is an out-come.

I am aware that what I am saying will seriously offend or even anger some folk, but that is not my intention. There can be a strong desire to know that an evil wrong-doer has been judged and sentenced to an eternity of pain and suffering - and I honestly get it. I have experienced that feeling myself, on behalf of poor souls who have fallen victim to acts of unbelievable horror. Certain news stories still haunt my mind, years after they occurred - and I can't unknow what I know. Some crimes are so awful that we instinctively cover our eyes or our ears when they are described to us, as if to ward them off. I am not ashamed to admit that I have fantasized about taking a gun to the heads of a few people over the years (always strangers to me) - but, unless it was a way of saving a life, I very much doubt that I would actually do it. On the other hand, what if the victim was someone dear to *me*? Who knows? I can't say for sure that I wouldn't (but then I'd have to face myself and my actions, beyond this life). I suppose my point is that punishment is not enough; in the history of mankind, there have probably been billions of souls who have been found guilty and sentenced to some form of penalty - whilst remaining utterly unrepentant and unremorseful. Imagine if their only hope of salvation was to experience exactly what they had inflicted upon others, and be sincerely horrified by their own intentions and behaviour? And that the only possible way to move beyond the claustrophobic, endless misery of their own energy (and the awfulness of the company of like-minded souls) is to be willing to take absolute responsibility - and to *choose* to evolve and make amends? Imagine the dawning realisation that the result of their lack of empathy is something that they can never slide away from or outrun? The thing about bullies and the generally cruel is that they are often too weak and cowardly to tolerate what they dish out to others. You may still disagree with me of course, but that's okay; I'd like to think that we wouldn't fall out over a difference of opinion! I am just explaining how I myself see it.

Here's an interesting story: a very long time ago, I was giving a consultation to a lady who wanted to hear from a man who had caused a lot of trouble and heartache for a number of people. At first, he seemed to be very apologetic, and I believed that he was sincere - for about five minutes. I cannot tell you why, but I suddenly and instinctively knew that he was playing a game, and the energy shifted from conciliatory to nasty. And, I was shocked when I was able to view his environment. He appeared to be in a dank, dirty, cold house, and the only piece of furniture was an old wooden chair. There were other buildings of a similar ilk, and the light was dull, grey, and misty... with the collective energy being one of misery and deprivation. I very swiftly ended the connection as I had no desire to open myself up to that particular horror. Now, as I said earlier, I am not suggesting that what I was seeing was an actual place, somewhere that could be pinpointed on a map; I think that it was probably more of an energetic reflection of a twisted soul's personal reality. It caused me to feel incredibly sad, because, after all, who would want to wish that upon anyone? Although it was a first for *me*, I did come across an old book written by a man who had worked as a medium, and in it he described a very similar experience, which I found fascinating. Fortunately, it hasn't been a common occurrence for me - but it certainly gave me something to ponder!

If you think about it, physical life pretty much operates along the same lines, when we human souls allow ourselves to become prisoners of our own mind, controlled by our own destructive perceptions and beliefs. Healing is only possible with a permanent change of mindset, which requires a willingness to challenge an out-of-control ego - which in turn requires courage. Of course, we only change *if* we really believe that we need and want to… and I imagine that that applies as much to the deceased as it does to the living!

Chapter 7

Does 'spirit' talk to us?

Well, yes, I believe that it does, but in whatever way we are wired to hear it. However, I probably should have started by saying that I feel the need to define what is *meant* by the term spirit, because it appears to mean different things to different people. To some, it seems to represent a bunch of nameless entities often referred to as 'they' - as in, "*they* are telling me this or that." I have often wondered who these souls are and *why* they pass on snippets of information that are basically chit-chat. Maybe it is just a friendly way of reaching out… a celestial version of Facebook! I have also heard 'spirit' being blamed for all manner of things and I have witnessed competition between groups of people to have the upper hand where spirit-connection is concerned! And, although this isn't exactly the same, it kind of runs along similar lines. I have worked with customers who have wanted to know exactly what their deceased relative *now* thinks about a particular person: *surely* they can see them in their true light now that they have the vantage point of being 'in spirit'! People have also wanted deceased relatives to reveal the location of money or possessions that have gone missing, following their passing. Sadly, even death isn't a guarantee of escape from sibling rivalry and family greed!

Generally speaking though, I believe that, apart from actual spiritual communication, we are receiving 'messages' from energetically non-physical beings on a consistent basis. I *have* recognised that a question I have asked of whoever-is-listening is being answered through a song I hear or words I find myself reading… because *I* love music and words and easily relate to them. And I have many, many questions, I can promise you! I have also been given information that I didn't ask for - and ignored or forgotten about until it became completely relevant, I am afraid to say. One such occasion, many years ago, was very sad: one of our dogs suddenly seemed a bit tired and sleepy, but I didn't immediately worry, thinking maybe it was just too warm for her. She was lying under the dining room table, and as I passed I clearly heard a voice in my head say, "Kim will die." I shook the thought away, thinking that it was something I had negatively cooked up myself, and pushed it to one side. That evening she lay down in front of the fire and went to sleep… and never woke up again. I tried to rouse her so I could let her out for a wee, and was absolutely devastated to find that she had quietly and silently passed away. I cannot say whether the words were generated by my own intuitive mind, or, in this case, by another source. As I have said, when I am 'tuning in' to another person or situation I believe I am using natural intuitive capacity, but I also believe that we do receive snippets of information and guidance from 'on high', as we go through our lives. Unfortunately, she'd seemed a little off-colour to me rather than ill, and I just didn't understand. I really don't know whether or not she could have been saved, but we would have been very short on time, anyway. She was an absolutely beautiful natured dog and is still very, very much missed (and yes, for those who wonder, *all* sentient beings have souls and their own kind of spirit… and we have already established that the soul does not die, or fade away like a thinning wisp of smoke drifting on the air. The spirit of Kim is still very much alive, in a dimension beyond human consciousness).

On a lighter note, sometimes a soul decides that, one way or another, they *are* going to be acknowledged and listened to! Recently, whilst I was recording a general consultation for a customer, (as an audio file to be delivered via email), I suddenly experienced a very sharp pain in the right side of my head. It caught my attention, which led me to become very much aware of a small, thin, elderly lady - who was now jabbing me in the shoulder with a fingernail! I have to admit that it rather annoyed me at first. She seemed pretty pushy and I briefly wondered if this was a 'dark' energy. However, I quickly realised that she was just incredibly determined to make herself known, because there was something that she wanted to say to my customer. She even apologised to me by giving me a little pat on the shoulder, and I understood that it was just her nature - and that she'd been a bit of a force to be reckoned with when physically alive. I can only assume that the pain in my head was the result of her intense focus - and I am glad that not all communications start that way! Anyway, once she had my attention, she was joined by a gentleman, and it was clear that they were aware of the general circumstances of my customer and were keen to offer well-intentioned advice and encouragement. They then left us to go about their own business - and I had a very strong sense that they were taking time and energy out of a busy schedule, in order to express their concern to a still-living relative! The funny thing is, I don't include spiritual communication with a general intuitive consultation. I wasn't looking to make any kind of link, and in fact was focusing my attention on the customer's work life (the main area of their concern). However, these two souls were pretty insistent!

Other souls cut in in different ways. I was lying in bed last night - well, it was actually early morning when this occurred - and, half awake, was pondering in which direction to take this book. This is a revised edition, but the existing book was starting to receive a number of low star ratings (not reviews), and I wasn't entirely sure why. Possibly because it isn't particularly long? Maybe some readers are offended by my personal views? Could it be because it is different to other books, written by popular, spiritualist mediums? Maybe some readers just don't like me, and don't enjoy my style or my 'voice'. But, what if it simply isn't good enough? Am I being true to the title, Our Life Beyond Death - An Incredible Journey: A Medium's Observations And Conclusions? (These are the kind of thoughts that go through every writer's mind, I imagine!) I felt that I needed to add something *more* - about what *I* feel to be true about the experience of life beyond physical death. Whilst I was chewing this over, a scene suddenly began to unfold upon the screen of my mind - of a young, black man, who was obviously a slave. I understood his name to be Joseph, and I heard the word 'Oklahoma'. I watched, as a stocky white man grabbed hold of him, yelling abuse - only for Joseph to snap, pushing the flat of his hand into the man's twisted face. The scene changed, and Joseph was on his back on the ground, and women were crying. My heart sank - I thought he was dead. However, the fingers of his left hand began to move, closing around a rock that was lying in the dirt beside him. I thought that he was going to get up and hit his attacker, and I feared for him... but he just lay there, as if calmly contemplating. And then, the scene changed, and Joseph was holding a bible - and I knew that he had read it from cover to cover and that he had great faith in it. I also understood that he eventually went on to become a preacher of some kind. However, I don't know what happened next; I think I drifted off to sleep for a few moments, because I lost the connection. I remembered that Joseph's last name began with B, but when I awoke this morning I couldn't bring it to mind. I liked him, he seemed intelligent, proud, and brave. I believe that he was trying to show me something, but am still pondering it. Newsflash! Whilst typing this, the penny has just dropped. He was telling me to have faith in the book! And he was also advising me that whilst it's okay to stand my ground, I can take the blows lying down - and be philosophical about it! Wow, thank you, Joseph, I appreciate it.

I do sometimes have little visits during the night, but I often fall asleep and have only vague memories the following morning - which is annoying! Recently, I heard "Robert... I used to take drugs" - and that's all I can remember. I don't recall a sense that this was a soul who was lost or in trouble; maybe he just wanted a chat. However, they need to show up a bit earlier if they hope to get anywhere with me!

I have heard mediums say that they can't shut off the voices of insistent spirits, but that isn't the case with me. I think that maybe it used to be - or, more likely, I was just willing to give my attention to every passing presence! For a long time I haven't wanted to be constantly open for business, especially if I am busy or tired. In fact, I think my reputation must go before me, because I don't tend to attract an endless stream of chatter from disembodied beings! One reviewer commented that I wasn't 'fully open to spirit', but I think that she meant *her* version of spirit, and *her* version of being open. I understood why she would make such a comment when I saw that she was a fan of one particular celebrity medium. However, that person and I are like chalk and cheese - in our beliefs, and the way in which we present our work... in my opinion at least. There are energies I don't want to become involved with, and I have probably created a kind of force field that causes them to pass me by. I suppose I am more likely to be 'visited' at night because my conscious mind is less in control. Even so, it has been a long time since I sensed anything threatening or unpleasant. So, if all of this is evidence of me not being fully open, I hold my hands up and admit to being guilty as charged!

I did have one particularly unsettling experience around twenty five years ago, which occurred late at night. We lived in an old terraced house, and, for some reason, I began to believe that there was something unpleasant linked to the stairs. I even heard a voice in my mind that said, "the man at the foot of the stairs is waiting for you", whilst lying in bed, struggling to sleep. I forced myself to get up and purposefully walk all the way to the bottom, terrified that something was going to reach out and grab me! Of course, it didn't. However, moments after I returned to bed, something quite scary *did* occur. I watched as an elderly man passed through the door and glided across the room. The expression on his face was strange; it was sad and heavy, and he appeared to be completely preoccupied. He didn't acknowledge me; in fact, I don't think he was even aware of my presence. And with him came the most unsettling sense of silence. Not just quietness - but cold, heart-stopping silence. And the oddest thing was, he was carrying some kind of sign, with words written upon it… but I couldn't read them. The whole thing was over and done with, in seconds, but it felt as though time had slowed down, making it seem much longer. I have never experienced anything like that since, and I honestly have no idea what it was all about. Strangely, even though it was like a scene from a scary ghost movie, I didn't feel that the old man had dark intentions. Thinking about it now, I believe that he probably *was* a ghost, rather than a non-physical soul (or spirit, if you prefer). Which is interesting, because that is a subject I have been thinking a lot about recently, in line with something else I am working on. Coincidence... or synchronicity?

Chapter 8

Ghosts and spirits: are they different?

The following is a blog post I published in 2018, expressing my negative views about ghost hunting:

Everyone is entitled to their opinion, and this is one of mine: there is absolutely nothing good to be said about ghost hunting.

I am not talking about those whose genuine work is connected to the healing or clearing of disturbing, destructive non-physical forms of 'energy'. I am talking about the deliberate intrusion of what are considered to be haunted venues, for the purpose of entertainment and titillation. It puts me in mind of jeering peasants who attended hangings and beheadings, throwing rotten vegetables at the unfortunate souls who were fearfully preparing to meet their maker.

So, what prompted me to write this blog post today? Well, a couple of nights ago, whilst trying to find something to watch on t.v., Dave came across a program called something like, 'My Ghost Story', and asked if I wanted to see what it was about. We thought it might be interesting, but it turned out to be just another set of stories about people who go marching into old prisons/hospitals/castles, armed with cameras and sound equipment, determined to make contact with a guy who hanged himself, or a woman who, grief-stricken over the death of her child, threw herself from a bedroom window. Nice.

And, of course, there was the usual dollop of mysteriously slamming doors, icy hands giving a shove from behind, weird shadows, orbs, and the recording of creepy, distorted, barely discernible 'voices', interpreted as threats and warnings. It reminded me just how repellent I find the whole ghost hunting thing, and it was peeing me off so much I could only stomach about 20 minutes of it... and that was 20 minutes too long!

It strikes me that some people believe that a ghost is different to a physically deceased soul... that they are two different species, not connected at all, which doesn't make sense. And I have never come across anyone who wants to think that their deceased loved one, or a deceased ancestor, is now a ghost, trapped in the hospital in which they died, or at the cemetery in which their body is laid to rest. I haven't worked with anyone who wants to believe that the friend or family member who took their own life is now stuck for eternity, reliving that moment again and again - and neither should they believe it. Just because a person died 50 or 100 years ago doesn't change a thing: guilty or innocent, they were still a soul who lived, loved and died. To demand and command that a potentially disturbed, angry, non-physical energy makes itself known, so that it can be provoked, questioned, and recorded, is downright nasty - and asking for trouble. If you go looking for the dark, be very careful what you wish for - you just might get it.

Let's face it, ghost hunting is never about having a nice chat with Auntie Alice, or about genuine, intelligent research; it is about drama and goading. Ghost hunters want to be scared, and to scare others. I have heard people say 'oh, but it is interesting!', or 'it's just a bit of fun!'. Okay, so go and read a good book, or take a course, or visit a theme park.

I was once asked to help out at an evening event, taking place in an old town hall. I really didn't have much information except that I would be one of three mediums; as it was a friend who had asked me I agreed and turned up as promised. I was surprised to see that most of the attendees had sleeping bags with them and it emerged that the event was actually an evening of ghost hunting, and that people were going to spend the whole night there. I quickly made my feelings known, and made it clear that I would stay for only a short while, overseeing the group I had been allocated, and that if anyone became frightened or upset, that would be it - I was gone. I wasn't taken seriously and most people, including my friend, laughingly dismissed much of what I said.

Fast forward 2 hours. Many attendees were crying and my friend decided that she didn't agree with ghost hunting after all. Not that anything dreadful happened, but in one of the halls in particular, there was a highly oppressive and unpleasant atmosphere (and of course the lights had been turned off), and the result was hysteria. Some claimed to have been touched by invisible hands, a few said that they had experienced strong feelings of sadness, and others were just vaguely terrified. I left them to their cups of tea and tears, and later learned that most of them wouldn't travel home alone and that, 2 weeks down the line, some were still sleeping with the bedroom light on! I admit that it was mean but I laughed, because I recognised that nothing really frightening or dangerous HAD happened, and that most of the attendees had actually terrified themselves; but still, had any of them been of a particularly vulnerable or fragile mindset, the experience could have triggered mental health problems. AND, if a not-so-benign energy had been present (attracted by the group's desire to dig up something dubious and dark), it would have found it easy to 'attach' itself to the easiest prey. I have definitely come across people to whom this has happened, regardless of what the cynics might say. You know what? To be on the safe side, just don't go there.

And there is nothing to say that the 'dark' energies that apparently inhabit the stereotypical haunted venues ARE the souls of deceased people who died there; who really knows for sure? I believe that there are many dimensions of awareness and that ours is just one, a teeny weeny part of something we couldn't even begin to measure; we probably aren't even a dot on a pinhead. And I believe that the dimensions - light/dark, evolved/unevolved - overlap one another to one degree or another... which is how 'hauntings' come about. And it wouldn't surprise me if our own dimension isn't sometimes spilling over into another dimension, making us the haunters, rather than the haunted.

I have, accidentally and unwittingly, experienced the effects of unfriendly entities, and I can tell you, I would go to the ends of the earth to avoid doing so again, unless there was absolutely no other choice. I remember the night I parked up outside of an old, crumbling house, desperate for peace and quiet and a bit of sleep. We lived in the middle of nowhere, a rural area with no street lights, and so you can imagine how dark it was. Our house was full of noise, and televisions, and computer games, and I was feeling exhausted. Leaving the children with their father, I decided to drive down the long dirt track, taking a blanket and a pillow with me, to find somewhere quiet enough for a snooze. The old, abandoned house was off-set, halfway down the track, and I parked up, facing the front. I got into the back seat, covered myself up, and was just dozing off when I felt it coming - something that could only be described as a ball of very threatening energy, heading directly my way. I shot up, intending to jump into the front seat, but I wasn't quick enough... it hit me, and passed straight through me, and you will never see anyone as desperate as I was to reverse out of an overgrown old lane, in the black of night! And I should have known better, because months earlier, a customer, trying to locate my house, told me that she'd stopped at the old cottage further down, to ask for directions. She'd noticed an old man looking out through the bedroom window, but he didn't respond to her knock. She realised that the place was dilapidated, but thought that that was just the way he lived.

When I told her that the house had been empty for years she was shocked! Whoever or whatever that energy was, it didn't want any intrusion from this physical dimension... and, recognising that something more than a person staring out of a window in an unfriendly manner was needed, in order to scare me off, it found a more effective way! I had no interest in digging around or going back for more, so it got its way!

I have also very occasionally picked up sounds and voices, whilst recording consultations (white noise), the most unsettling being one that sounded like "help me". I asked a number of people, including my children, to listen and verify that I wasn't imagining it (and they were all a bit freaked out), before passing it onto a friend who was part of a healing circle. She and her associates focused on assisting and encouraging the whispering soul to move on... but then the recording suddenly disappeared, never to be found again. At first, I was really disappointed to lose what I saw as paranormal evidence (even though it made me sad to hear that voice) until I realised that there was no longer a need for it. I have heard that collective prayer can be incredibly powerful, and I think that maybe the motivation, the intention, and the will of that healing circle was enough to lovingly assist a lost soul to find its way forward.

Having said that, not all paranormal activity is the work of an actual entity. Strong emotion, especially fear, rage, and grief, can leave something of itself behind - a tangible residue that can, in turn, react to the strong emotions of the living. Who can say why certain places/buildings/items are more receptive than others, and who can say why certain human souls are more aware than others? But what I do know for sure is that if the intention is to seek out the dark - the misery, suffering, and anguish that has been imprinted upon the face of time, like an insidious tape recording - in an attempt to conjure up the souls of those who might possibly 'haunt' the last, desperate place they experienced on earth, it really is pretty questionable behaviour. As I said at the start, everyone is entitled to their opinion - and this is mine!

I am now going to re-examine a statement I made early on in the post:

"It strikes me that some people believe that a ghost is different to a physically deceased soul... that they are two different species, not connected at all, which doesn't make sense."

I am going to agree and disagree - with myself! I know what I was trying to convey, which is, if you have lost someone that you love, would you be happy to imagine them forever revisiting the location of their death? Of course not. But then, our deceased loved ones are different - aren't they? They aren't like these dark entities who hang around creepy buildings or graveyards... or even hospitals, or the road/street upon which they met their death. And so, from that point of view, we separate the ghosts from the spirits. And, because we have no emotional attachment to the ghost, we can view it dispassionately. It's a bad and scary thing, to be poked and aggravated, for the sake of entertainment or self-promotion - not like our beloved ones (regardless of the nature of their passing). Now, I still believe that all of this is true. However, I was wrong, when I said that it doesn't make sense to see ghosts and spirits as two different species; well, partially wrong, at least. I was so keen to remind people that the 'ghosts' they are hunting for fun may well be someone else's lost loved one, or even an ancestor, that I failed to go as far with it as I could. And actually, I do believe that, in some cases, ghosts are ghosts, and not spirits (in the way in which we understand them).

As I have previously mentioned, I believe that there are many, many other dimensions of existence - millions, billions, trillions? Who could possibly know for sure? If that assumption is true, then it is probably naive to attempt to simplify the subject by creating just two categories: Ghosts, and Spirits. However, if we are exploring it superficially, I would say that a ghost is a cold energy, and a spirit a warm one; a ghost comes with a sense of lifelessness and joylessness, whilst a spirit produces an energy that is 'alive'; some ghosts are possibly echoes or recordings, or the result of powerful, trapped feelings and emotions; spirits are more sentient and responsive. Are all ghosts 'bad' and all spirits 'good'? Again, I don't believe that it can be so easily categorised. But, for now, that is all I am going to say on the subject - because I want to save the rest for my new book!

Chapter 9

It's me again...

The following was a post I published on my Facebook author's page, fairly recently:

I was working through my list of consultations a couple of days ago, and I had been asked to check if a particular deceased loved one was 'around'. I sat quietly, with my eyes closed, gazing into the soft, endless darkness, and brought the person in question to mind. Almost immediately I was able to 'see' him, and I waited for the communication to begin. You have to listen with your mind, and pay attention to the images that flit across the screen of the mind (or, at least, that's how it works for me). The biggest question in my mind was "what is he actually doing now... how is he feeling, and what is happening with him?" I understood that this soul had had some

pretty tough times throughout his life, and had been really reflecting upon his incarnation and his own choices and actions. He hadn't been gone for long, and it seems that he had been experiencing a form of energetic healing - but was now ready to move forward (I suppose you could describe it as going to the next level, although it is probably more complex than that). He shared a number of his thoughts with me, which I then shared with the customer, and he really wanted to let her know that, even though he was now expanding his horizons, he would still be within reach for her. He was incredibly concerned for her emotional welfare, assuring her that he would always stay connected to her.

But, still, I wanted to know what he was actually seeing and experiencing, and I found myself caught up in a dreamy meditation... gazing into what I can only describe as clouds of colour (soft and rich in tone, rather than bright), that changed shape and form, even presenting faces that appeared briefly before melting away. It felt peaceful, yet incredibly vibrant and 'alive'. I asked how painful it is to leave loved ones behind - and I experienced a pang of sadness, that was swiftly replaced by a completely comforting understanding that "they will be fine", and a knowingness that, energetically speaking, even though a physical incarnation can seem to be a lengthy experience, in reality, it passes by in the blink of an eye.

I found myself opening my eyes and coming back to 'earth' - and everything looked so clear and beautiful! I was struck by the miracle of life in this physical world, and how amazing it is! And then, all of a sudden, I experienced the energy of the customer herself, and was hugely saddened by the sense of overpowering heaviness and hopelessness she was struggling with. I understood exactly why her lost loved one was so concerned for her and hoped that the consultation would help her a little. And, funnily enough, whilst typing this, I received an email from her: "Thank you for telling me about him. It breaks my heart, but also gives me some peace of mind that he's still around." As for myself, I cannot say that I know what he is doing... but at least I know what he is feeling, which is probably more important.

Before writing this chapter, I once again asked, "what does the experience of being 'dead' feel like?" (I am like a mithering child, asking the same question over and over again). I closed my eyes, cleared my mind, and waited. I became aware of a presence sitting beside me on the sofa, and I heard, "there is light. There is sense - you can feel. There is touch and sensation. There is motion. There are pathways and branches. There are bridges. The heart is clear, and becomes clearer." This was followed by what I can only describe as an understanding: I felt that I would be aware of a source of pure, endless knowledge; I felt that I would be aware of a natural, energetic connection to kindred souls - and not just those with whom I shared an incarnation, but those with whom I resonate, and have a desire to learn from; I felt that I would experience absolute appreciation for my life, and an overwhelming sense of love for those who still remained; I felt that I would create my own reality, little by little... that it would be like a bird unfolding its wings before learning to fly, or a flower budding before opening its petals to the elements. I don't know the source of these insights, and I didn't ask. It didn't seem important, somehow. All I needed to do was to open my mind and listen. And I think that the pathways and branches are probably choices and experiences to be explored; that the bridges are maybe links between levels of awareness and progression; that the heart is obviously not a physical organ, but the living, feeling part of us. It helped me to adjust my filter, which was a blessed relief... and I will explain what I mean.

I had forgotten to view non-physical life in a non-physical way. I was looking for black and white answers, hoping to be able to cross the t's and dot the i's. I don't know how I got into that mindset - or maybe I do. Thinking about it, it was because I had become worn down and jaded. Several of our beloved pets passed within a very short space of time, mostly because they were of a similar age. I knew that one day it would happen, but wasn't prepared for the reality. My youngest daughter's grief was even greater than my own - or maybe I am able to handle it a little better, courtesy of age, experience, and beliefs. To witness her devastation and heartbreak, and not be able to do a thing to ease her pain, was incredibly difficult. There were other things, too, not least the effects of the pandemic (I am adding this chapter since originally publishing this book), and the unrest that swept across the planet. I watched as the situation brought out the best and the worst in people, unpleasantly surprised by the behaviour of certain individuals - especially a few who are fond of trotting out spiritual platitudes on social media. Their vitriolic rage and their willingness to promote conspiracy theories - without engaging in genuine, honest research beforehand - sickened me. I am not perfect and can rant with the best of them, but their intention was to blacken the names and reputations of certain others, and upset and worry vulnerable, anxious people - in order to fit their own agenda. I am all for a fair, honest fight, and for standing up for what we believe in - but the lines can become dangerously blurred, especially when ignorance is involved. Every time I was presented with 'facts' that should have me joining a lynch mob or running for the hills, I went into research-mode, and was appalled by how much was being edited and distorted. I was very lucky throughout the lockdown period; I live in a beautiful part of the world, and, in comparison to many other locations, we were fairly safe. I work from home anyway, and so my life wasn't really disrupted. I have family members who still had to go out to work, due to the nature of their jobs, and my eldest daughter's business could not operate (although she managed to livestream some of it from home); however, on the whole, it definitely could have been worse. On reflection, the toughest part for me was the ways in which people appeared to change. My daughter showed me how to mute people on social media - rather than offend them by blocking them - which was a blessed relief (the odds on myself having been muted by others are sky-high!), and I reminded myself to steer clear of stuff that would anger and depress me. I have never, ever wanted to run away from the reality of the world and live in a cozy bubble, but it was starting to seriously affect me, mentally and emotionally. I now recognise that I'd lost touch with something important, and had started to view existence through sad, angry, weary eyes; I forgot about the bigger picture and just wanted 'answers' that would give me instant relief... but all that that did was to make me feel worse. And that is how I got into that mindset! I recognise that I need to have a foot in each of two camps: 1) this physical life experience; 2) another, in which I, the human soul, am connected to something greater than myself. The truth is, I had stumbled, and both of my feet had landed in the one-dimensional quicksand of 'real' life. I just had to get myself out of it - and my gentle, anonymous messenger certainly helped me.

Chapter 10

Our spiritual DNA

There was a bright, talented young man who died suddenly and tragically. I knew him from watching him on television as an up-and-coming racing driver, but didn't *know* him. Feeling rather intrusive, I opened my mind and asked if it was possible to have a quick chat with him. And, I did link with him, in my usual way, briefly. What I understood was that his immediate concern was for his family and friends... but that he *also* experienced a great sense of wonderment. In life, he was committed to his sport, paying keen attention to detail - and I just knew that, in 'death', he was aware of the presence of his heroes who had gone before him, and that he would continue to absorb knowledge, and to create, in line with his passion. Because that was who he was - and still *is*... and because it is what he chooses for himself. He will continue to earn his right to have access to all that he needs for his own personal evolution.

You see, everything has to exist energetically *before* it can exist physically. Everything that has been created and produced by mankind *had* to start out as an idea in someone's mind. I believe that all ideas and inventions are plucked, albeit unconsciously, from the great creative store of life. I know that I have already spoken about this, but a bit of repetition can't hurt! Every single human experience is a very precious commodity, and is always absorbed by the collective soul, following each individual death. You can imagine the energy of the passionate, expressive, competitive, and brave young soul, can't you? And, you can imagine the wisdom of the mature, long-lived, contemplative soul, too. What is deposited can always be withdrawn, though it will still require something from ourselves, and will still demand commitment and effort. We might not know it, but every sudden, inspirational idea we have is never our own; however, we can shape and form it so that it *becomes* our own - a new version of the original. And, when we die, the spirit that we have created, that contains a record of all of our endeavours, will be absorbed by the collective store of knowledge - and someday, somewhere on the planet, someone will benefit from *our* contribution - without ever having met us!

Or, we might suddenly align ourselves with something that unconsciously resonates with us at a deeper level. Many years ago, I was lying in an overly warm hotel room, sniffling and flu-ridden, when an idea popped into my mind. It led me to become involved in the world of publishing, and to produce a relatively successful magazine, without any previous experience. Okay, it took me two years to get it off the ground, with many twists and turns along the way... but I did it. Where did that inspiration come from? Was it my higher self who knew that I had that ability within me? Or, was I tapping into a creative source of energy that was just waiting for me to pay attention? I certainly hadn't set out to achieve that particular goal, and yet the idea of it presented itself to me. It was then up to me to explore it or ignore it. I believe that we all have spiritual DNA, (although that might be an odd way of describing it!), and that we are all born with curiosity, passion, and talent written within us - that is unique *to* us.

Unfortunately, the world is still evolving, and there is much that we haven't yet learned to recognise and understand. We have come up with a limited number of boxes into which human beings are supposed to fit, otherwise they are deemed 'wrong', or in need of fixing. Billions of human souls will live and die without ever really knowing the joy of developing their own interests and ideas, and of turning their talent into skill - because of fear of not being good enough, and of social judgement. We are always being told that we have to be responsible and place the idea of security above everything else; that there are certain pastimes that shouldn't be taken too seriously because they won't pay the bills. I remember the young girl who came to see me, struggling with her career pathway - and I just knew that what she was studying was making her miserable, because it wasn't what she really wanted to do. I asked her why. "I wanted to pursue art, as I love to repair and renovate things… but my father said that there was no money in it and that I had to choose something that would give me security." I understood that his intentions were well-meaning, but I still wanted to shake him! I replied, "are you kidding? Has he not noticed how popular upcycling has become… and how much money there is to be made from it?" She just looked sad, because it was clear that he didn't believe in her - and so she stopped believing in herself. But, I can promise you one thing: if she lives her entire incarnation without adequately expressing herself through art, she will be unfulfilled and dissatisfied - because she came into this world with an inbuilt, earned passion for something that is crying out to be embraced (and she wouldn't possess it in the first place if she *hadn't* earned it). You might say, "well, she could paint as a hobby", and I would say, "yes, she *could* - but experience has taught me that, if she is like most people, she won't." This is because life takes over; we become consumed by it all, especially when we aren't engaged in what really inspires us. We become tired, and then we think, "oh, what's the point? It'll never get me anywhere, anyway."

Doesn't it make you feel sad, to think about the eager human souls who enter into this world equipped with something interesting that is unique to them... only to discover that it is viewed - by many of their fellow human beings - as valueless? I do accept that, for many of us, it can take years for us to understand what really excites us, or to recognise our 'calling'; however, the signs will usually be there. As a child, I loved reading and writing, dancing, and listening to music. No-one taught me to love those things - they were just natural to me. I wrote a lot of stories, as a teenager, before drifting off on the tide of life. It was never something that was going to pay the bills - or so I assumed. No-one ever told me that it *could*. I wanted to take dance lessons but my mother couldn't afford them, and so I made do with playing record after record, as I leapt around the room. I ended up working for an insurance company, before taking a better paid office job. I was always late, and always in trouble... because it just wasn't *me*. I eventually came back to writing, making room for it alongside my 'day job', and all of the usual domestic stuff. And that's exactly how it will work for most of those amongst us who eventually choose to honour their spiritual DNA. However, could we be more encouraging to our *younger* souls, so that they don't have to repeat our own frustrated patterns? I reckon that we could.

The young man I mentioned earlier was a soul who *did* follow his natural calling - with a lot of support, but also because of the belief that certain others had in him. Not every young person who has the desire and the potential skill to become a motor racing driver will make it; it costs money, and there are limited places. But, they could be helped to at least explore that world and all of the wonderful, associated opportunities. Sadly, his natural calling also led to his physical death - but he will be ever remembered, and important lessons *will* be learned. And, not only that, in his name, others will be given a chance to develop their own potential. I don't know what his family feel and believe; they obviously recognise that he died doing something that he completely loved. Maybe they sadly accept that and are reassured by it; maybe they regret it. I seriously hope that it is the former, rather than the latter, for their own peace of mind. They deserve and are owed that, at the very least.

To finish this chapter, I want to add that we don't have to be the absolute best at something in order for it to be our calling.

There will always be writers who occupy the place reserved for 'the greats', and it is highly unlikely that I will ever get to join them there - and yet I *still* feel compelled to tap away at those laptop keys! Whatever we develop and nurture in this incarnation will be ours to keep, and will become part of us when we leave this world. And, it doesn't need to be obvious or heroic; we might be naturally witty and funny; we might be great at hill-walking... or baking, or gardening, or negotiating. It could be anything. All it has to do is to provide us with a sense of satisfaction and achievement - and leave us wanting more! It is our spiritual legacy, and we should absolutely claim it and embrace it.

Chapter 11

A thought about angels

(originally published in A Little Slice Of Comfort Food)

I love the idea of angels - and I definitely believe that there are many different forms of non-physical being. I am just not sure that they exist in the way that they are popularly portrayed. However, it doesn't really matter, because that's what's so wonderful about all things 'spiritual': we each have our own beliefs - and if something feels real to *us*, then it *is* real! If we believe that angels have wings and a halo, then that is how they will appear to us. If we believe that they leave feathers around for us to find, as little gifts, signs, or messages, then that is what will happen. We always receive 'communications' in whatever way happens to resonate with us, personally. Well, that's what I think, anyway.

But, here's an interesting little story, about something that took place during the summer, in our small, suntrap of a back garden. I was relaxing in one of the two patio chairs, enjoying the sight and scent of an abundance of potted plants, flowers, and herbs... when I suddenly became aware that I was not alone. A petite figure, in a lavender-coloured, cap-sleeved dress, was sitting in the other chair - and she was busily sewing. She smiled, impishly, when it became clear that I was aware of her presence - and I swear that I could taste and smell the sweetness of parma violet! Her short hair was adorned with fresh flowers, and her long dress was similarly awash with flowers and butterflies. I cannot remember at all what we chatted about - it is a source of great frustration to me that I appear to enter into a kind of waking-trance state when I am having these little conversations - and that most of what is communicated disappears from my conscious mind very quickly. Anyway, what I do remember is that she introduced herself as Lydia... and that she was a bundle of pure, unadulterated joy! Happiness, pleasure, and humour poured from her, as did her love of nature. I can't even remember how we parted company. It was probably some distraction from the physical world that broke the 'spell', I imagine. I have thought about her many times since then - but I cannot say whether she was an angel, or something like a nature spirit. Either way, it was a really nice experience!

So, even though I cannot say that I see angels in exactly the same way that others do, I have enjoyed writing about them. In celebration of them, I would like to share with you two short poems I wrote several years ago, and I hope that you enjoy them. (P.S. I definitely believe in earth angels because I am lucky enough to have been bailed out by them *many* times throughout my life!)

Loving Angels

When loving angels walk with you,

They tread with step so light,

You never know they're with you,

And you never see the light.

When loving angels touch you,

To gently reassure,

You never hear the whispered words,

"I'm here for evermore."

Yes, loving angels let you be,

Whilst others criticise,

For loving angels only see

With truly loving eyes.

Your Angel

No matter who or what you be,

Your angel loves you endlessly.

No act, no crime, no sin or flaw,

Can keep your angel from your door.

Forgive yourself and others too -

That's what your angel wants for you.

A life of love, of growth and gain,

Through sunny days, through hail and rain.

Your angel made a promise friend,

To be with you until the end.

So, see yourself as angels do,

And then you'll know why they love you.

Chapter 12

A bran tub of stories

A few days ago, I decided to try and make a connection with my father. My childhood was not a mentally and emotionally easy one, and we didn't have a great relationship. I hadn't even seen or spoken to him for some time before his passing, but I believe that he had become quite frail. I did feel sad for him (despite the fact that my last visit with him ended with me being virtually thrown out by the scruff of my neck!), because he'd lost his beloved dog and his adored wife - who had been the only ones he'd *really* cared about - long before he himself passed; despite having other family members around, especially my younger half-sister (who, quite frankly, deserves a medal), he must have been so lonely. In connecting with him, I wasn't looking for anything other than a sense of what he is currently experiencing. Almost immediately, a little scene unfolded upon the screen of my mind, and I watched as he engaged in outdoor work, moving stones around, as if he was creating something. He and my stepmother had had a smallholding, and they were forever outdoors, growing this and building that, so it didn't surprise me... but it pleased me. And then I heard his bossy voice in my head: "write things down!" At the time, I *was* feeling muddled and under pressure, with a million things to do, and so it made perfect sense, given the way that he himself went about things. I chuckled to myself, and left it at that. I just knew that my stepmother was somewhere in the background, and probably too all of the dogs they had loved and lost.

I also decided to do the same thing with my mother, even though I don't actually think about her in that way; she always feels more like a child to me than an authority figure. All I saw was an image of her, as a young woman, sitting in the grass and gazing out across a green and pleasant landscape, her black hair tumbling down her back, and her skirt long and flowing. She looked pretty, and at peace. My mother was a free spirit - a bit of a loose cannon, in many ways. She was interesting, and intelligent - but certainly lacking in common sense and staying power. I can see aspects of her within myself, alongside those from my father - something which has proved to be good *and* bad! They were a disaster waiting to happen. Technically, they should never have gotten together. I believe that they had only known each other for around three weeks before tying the knot - and they ended up driving each other crazy. I have often wondered who I would be if two *other* human souls had brought me into the world instead of them - and also, how I would have turned out if they had actually loved each other and created a stable family life. I am not sure that I would be the person I am today (and some might say that that would be a good thing!); I might not look at the world in the way that I do if things had been easier and more predictable. I can honestly say that I wouldn't choose to go back and experience it all again... but, thinking about it now, I might not actually change anything, either.

Reflecting upon my childhood, I can see that I had some degree of natural intuitive capacity, although there was no psychic granny or aunt reassuring me that I had inherited the family 'gift' - thank goodness! I believe that it was more productive for me to have to figure it all out for myself, developing knowledge and skills in my own way. I didn't even really pay much attention to it until my early twenties, when I explored the idea of mediumship and life after death, before wandering off again, finally coming back to it when I was in my mid thirties. Although sincerely interested in learning more, I became repelled by the 'industry', and all of the dubious antics I witnessed. My stepsister and I started to attend a spiritualist church in Manchester, eventually joining the development class. On one hand, this is where it became clear to me that I did have some degree of clairvoyant ability; on the other hand, it also became clear to me that there are some pretty weird and unscrupulous people out there! Some of the claims that were being made were ludicrous, and I will never forget the woman who was invited to channel her spirit guide for our group - and who immediately adopted an obviously put-on voice with a very bad accent, pretending to be someone called Jenny who used to work in the mills in Lancashire. The stuff she came out with would have seriously upset some people, especially those who had lost loved ones in a particular war. I expressed my disgust to the president of the church, and was told, "oh well, I know... but she's harmless. And anyway, she didn't charge us, so it didn't cost us anything!" Really? *That's* your concern? And, when they invited a so-called spiritual healer to demonstrate his ability, and he knelt in front of a mortified-looking young woman (who clearly felt that she shouldn't make a fuss), making strange noises as he ran his hands up the insides of her legs, I knew it was time to re-think the whole thing. Of course, the rest of us almost choked, trying to stifle our embarrassed laughter - but it wasn't funny, especially for her. Now, I am *not* suggesting that all spiritualist churches operate in this way. I think that the couple who were in charge of that particular outfit were probably just delusional and a bit crazy. They were struggling with their relationship, amongst other things, and if it wasn't one of them moaning to the group, it was the other. Sadly, she developed a number of health issues and passed at a fairly young age (after which, for a short while, my stepsister was afraid to sleep in case she 'haunted' her, which goes to show just how dark the whole situation had become). I am not saying that neither of them possessed mediumistic ability; I believe that *he* did, for sure, but he was clearly battling a number of inner demons, and it was not the best introduction to the world of 'spirit' for a twenty-two year old!

Having said all of that, I do have a positive story to tell about 'him' (I should give him a name... let's make it Joe). The last time I saw Joe was some time after my niece had died. He had called at my house and I was telling him how sad I was feeling. I went to make a cup of tea, and when I returned he started to tell me all about her. "I can see her dressed in yellow", he said, which didn't impress me, because on the arm of my chair lay a photo of her when she was a bridesmaid at my wedding - and her dress was yellow! Sadly, on the same day that my niece died, one of my beloved cats was killed on the road outside our house. Joe told me that she was telling him, "I have the *real* cat, and she can have the pot cat." I had no idea what pot cat he was talking about, and the conversation moved on to other things. Later that day, I went to visit my sister - and as I walked through the living room door, the very first thing that caught my attention was a little black and white pottery cat, sitting on the shelf directly above the bed in which my niece had - in a coma-type state - been lying (meaning that she could not have been consciously aware of it). I had never noticed it before, even though it must have always been there. And, I later found out that on the day she *technically* died (whilst out for fresh air, in her wheelchair), she was dressed all in yellow. I made a mental apology to Joe because he had been right after all. But, given all that had happened, I suppose you *can* understand my distrust! It's all just grist for the mill, isn't it? And at least it gave me something to write about!

Now, here's an amusing little story about a pub, a power cut, and a priest! I had forgotten all about it until just now. I had taken a booking from a group of people who wanted to have individual consultations, and the event was to take place in an old public house. The only thing about that evening that stands out in my mind was the crashing thunderstorm that developed as I was working with one of the group - which caused the lights to suddenly go out, plunging us into absolute darkness - at which point I suddenly became very aware that an angry looking priest was glaring in my direction! I nearly jumped out of my skin, and started feeling around the table for my customer's hand, whimpering "are you still there?" Luckily, the lights came back on within minutes, and I apologised for my response, explaining about our unfriendly-looking visitor. She wasn't at all surprised, telling me that the building had once been a church, many moons ago. We laughed about it, but I felt pretty silly. However, in my defence, a combination of thunder, darkness, and the sudden appearance of a cross old man would probably spook anyone! And now, I am duty bound to address the question: ghost or spirit? I would say spirit, because he appeared and felt very 'real'. I am sure that, in his world, the building was still a church, and therefore the presence of someone like me was probably a huge intrusion to him. I really had no interest in digging any deeper, and anyway, there was no need. Live and let live, I say (or, in this case, live and let die!).

On a more sombre note, some years ago a psychic made an appointment to see me - and I was quite shocked when it became clear just how much of a mess she was. Mentally and emotionally exhausted, she was a bag of nerves and blistering with resentment - especially toward her 'gift', which, she bitterly informed me, had ruined her life. She had made a series of disastrous choices where her love life was concerned, and some of the problems she was facing were clearly overwhelming her. Even typing this takes my breath away, as I remember the dark cloud that seemed to have a hold on her. Although I had heard of her, I had never met her, and I recall that she was generally well regarded - despite the fact that she had a habit of cancelling customers at the last minute, working under more than one name, and having random periods of time out. The weight of it all was too much for her, and she told me that people only wanted her for her gift, which strengthened my belief that the idea of certain individuals being 'special' in a psychic way is not a good thing. I see it as an ability, a skill that can be developed - and one that requires us to expand our horizons in a whole host of ways. She was clearly vulnerable, highly sensitive, and had fallen prey to the wrong kind of energies for her. I did try to help her, and she said that she would come and see me again… but I never heard from her after that. The psychic/spiritual industry is not all sweetness and light, by any stretch of the imagination, and those of us who are doing our best to operate from an honest and well-intentioned place need to take care of ourselves. I genuinely wish her well and hope that she managed to gain some peace of mind, and find happiness. And I also hope that she left the psychic work behind - it wasn't doing her any good at all.

Chapter 13

Our Loved Ones Stay In Touch...

(originally published in A Little Slice Of Comfort Food)

The young woman was in her early thirties when she passed, and her devastated mother was desperate for reassurance. "I just need to know that she's alright, and to tell her that we love her," she explained. As soon as I opened myself to the connection, her daughter appeared upon the screen of my mind, smiling, and waving. She showed herself on a wide, sandy beach, and was dressed in jeans and a baggy, roll-neck jumper; in the background people were laughing and playing, and the air was alive with the chatter of joyful souls. It was fairly brief, but almost as if she was making a video call, rather than presenting herself as 'present' in the room. However, there was no mistaking the fact that she appeared to be perfectly okay; and, of course, there was no need to reassure her that she was dearly loved - she already knew that and was able to feel every single ounce of it! I don't know why she showed herself on a busy, sun-kissed beach... but my feeling is that she wanted to express to her loved ones that she was doing just fine, and that they shouldn't worry.

****

They loved their father, even though he had been a stubborn, sometimes grumpy soul. As I connected with him, I noticed that he was holding a banana skin in his hand - and I had absolutely *no* idea what he was trying to communicate! I explained what I was seeing, and his daughter laughed out loud. "My brother hates bananas," she explained, "but my father would still make him eat them. At his funeral, when we were each dropping a flower into the grave, I whispered to my brother that maybe he should be throwing a banana skin in, instead!" Apparently, the 'dead' attend their own funeral services... and this beloved dad was letting them know that he'd overheard her little joke!

****

She was heartbroken because no-one had been with her father when he passed; the family had spent the day at his bedside, but had nipped out to have something to eat - and while they were gone, he quietly slipped away. Overcome with feelings of guilt, she wanted to apologise to him, and let him know how much she missed him. Of course, there was absolutely no need for her to feel so bad, as he explained to me, using his familiar, dry sense of humour: "tell her not to worry - it's not a spectator sport!" In other words, he'd wanted to save them from having to witness his passing.

****

The young woman's mother was looking for a way to reassure her daughter that it definitely *was* her we were communicating with. Whilst 'tuning in', I began to taste something, though at first I couldn't pinpoint what it was. And then it clicked with me: sugared almonds! The girl was delighted. "My mother absolutely loved them," she exclaimed. "In fact, her loud crunching used to drive me mad - and so she'd do it all the more!"

****

She'd been a very house proud lady, and as I connected with her, the smell of soap was almost overwhelming. However, it wasn't flowery - it was the almost clinical scent of those big green bars that used to look like small bricks... and left the skin feeling as if it had been well and truly scrubbed! They quickly recognised her as their beloved, bustling grandmother - and they definitely remembered the soap!

****

Pat's Story

Pat was 94 when she left this world, having lived with Alzheimer's disease for a number of years. As we connected, I was struck by how much younger she felt to me; although I know that non-physical souls often present themselves as younger and fitter than they were at the time of their passing, this was different. It was as if she was younger than her age *before* she died, despite her health challenges! She was a very down to earth lady, with a warm sense of humour, and showed me images of herself as a younger woman… and it was clear to me that she'd been attractive, well-turned-out, and energetic. She communicated how she had been, just prior to her passing, and I watched as a scene unfolded upon the screen of my mind, of her departing her body - and as she did so, she lovingly thanked it for its service, which really touched me. I don't believe that I had ever seen that before. Just before the consultation ended, Pat said, "stop taking things so seriously", which I duly reported - before suddenly realising that she was talking to *me*, not her daughter! And she was right; I had been feeling a bit bogged-down and joyless, allowing the dramas of the world to get to me. As I thanked her, I felt her move in close to me and place a firm kiss on my forehead… and then she was gone. It was a lovely experience, and I was really pleased that I had 'met' her! A few days later, I received an email from her daughter, which I would like to share with you - not to blow my own trumpet, because I never want my work to be about *me* - but because I think that it adds something to Pat's story:

Thank you so much for this wonderful consultation, Leanne. My goodness, you just got it soooo incredibly right.

Having been mum's carer for the past 15 years, I became intricately acquainted with every nuance of her physical condition and needs, because I had to sort everything out for her in a medical sense! So, your description of these things was just so spot on. And also, regarding when she passed. I was there with her right up to the end when we were together in the emergency ward at the hospital, so I know just how it was. I particularly understand when you mentioned she said 'Thank you' to her body for doing such a great job! That amazing body of hers went through, and recovered resplendently from, many hard times in these past years - we were all in complete awe of her resilience and ability to recover.

*But, most importantly, you really got the **essence** of this gorgeous woman and picked up so beautifully on what a great character she was - she was all of those things you said and very much a people person, who had a number of very close, lifelong friends - but also, all my friends (and my brother's friends) adored her because she was very young at heart (and also wise), and **hugely** relatable. I'm not one bit surprised to hear you say at the end of the recording that she was talking to you, and I could tell it was with a sense of familiarity, which is very much her style. She was just so like that as a human being. I love her to pieces and I am so grateful to you for doing this.*

Take care and all my best wishes,

G x

****

I stepped off the last bus of the evening, exhausted, and not looking forward to the longish walk home through the dark and lonely streets. This was in the days when I worked full-time hours in the sales department of a radio station, before heading off on public transport to attend group bookings all over the city. I needed to make it back to the railway station for the last train, and in order to be able to catch the connecting bus for home... but I didn't always make it. One minute too late was enough to leave me in the position of having to spend at least half of my earnings on a taxi (which wasn't ideal, as I was the family's main breadwinner); however, on this particular evening, I *did* make it. As I said, I wasn't relishing the journey, worrying that some crazy person might jump out and hit me over the head - until I became aware that I wasn't alone after all. My companion was an elderly man who appeared to be gliding along beside me, and I somehow understood that he had lost his legs at some point in his old life. He talked to me about the history of the area, and about the years he spent working at a mine, which was absolutely fascinating. When we reached the corner of my street, he nodded goodbye, and went on his way. I never did discover the identity of my protector, but I genuinely appreciated his company!

****

He wanted to let her know that he was truly sorry for having let her down, for not being the kind of father he should have been.

He communicated that he understood that she might not want to hear from him, but that he would always be within reach if she ever needed to talk to him. I felt that he was sincere, and I also understood that maybe the past had not been as clear-cut as she had been led to believe; there are, after all, often two sides to a story. He acknowledged that he could have done better, but that his intention had never been to wilfully shut her out. He and her mother just couldn't seem to get along, and there was so much bitterness toward him that he took the coward's way out and stayed away. Now he wished that he had behaved differently, and even though it was too late, he was working on healing himself, and he wanted to let her know that he had always loved her. Although she struggled to accept the communication, I could see that it was reaching her, and that it was providing a little relief from the hurt and the anger. She wasn't about to completely forgive him… but at least it was a starting point.

****

I pointed to a lady in the audience (I will call her Anne), and explained that I could 'see' an elderly woman standing close behind her. As is always the way, I had no idea who she was, but at least I was able to describe her. It emerged that she was a grandmother - who had consistently favoured two other family members over

Anne (who had done everything for her), despite the fact that they rarely bothered with her. It also emerged that those same family members were also present, but seated at another table... and the underlying resentments were pretty obvious. Anne had been incredibly hurt by her grandmother's attitude, but she continued to take care of her until the very end. I understood why the woman chose to connect specifically with Anne that evening, and I explained why. Her grandmother had done what so many others have: she bit the hand that fed her, taking the love and kindness for granted - because she could. *And* because she was unhappy with life and had nothing better to do. It was unfair and unreasonable... and she knew it. She wanted to let her granddaughter know that she was sorry, and that she appreciated her - and what better way to do that than in front of those she had wrongly placed above Anne, in her affections? The past can never be repaired or altered, but, despite her apparent indifference, I *did* notice a satisfied little smile dancing around the edges of Anne's mouth - and quite rightly so.

****

I had been asked to provide a consultation for a well-known singer and actor, and was kindly given tickets for one of his shows. During the performance, I became aware that a guy was sitting on one of the large speakers at the front of the stage, looking relaxed, and clearly enjoying the music. He seemed to be aware that I was watching him, and rubbed his stomach, knowing that I would pick up on it. When I described this man to my celebrity customer, he instantly recognised him as his road manager - who had recently passed as a result of stomach cancer. He obviously knew that I would be speaking to his old boss, and wanted to let him know that he was still around!

****

Nina's Story

Nina contacted me via Facebook messenger, when she heard that I was writing this book. She had a story that she really wanted to share with me… and I was absolutely delighted to receive it! And, as requested, I will let her tell it in her own words:

"This might not be of any help, but it's definitely one reading that has stayed in my mind. I'm just going to write it as I would say it, if that's ok?

I wasn't even supposed to have a reading that day. I was working in the takeaway, downstairs, and you were doing readings for a group of my boss's friends. Fortunately for me, one didn't turn up and so I was offered the space.

I remember walking into the kitchen to see you sitting at the table, and as this was my first ever reading I was nervous and didn't know what to expect. You asked me to sit across from you, and began almost straight away.

You told me that there was a man standing behind me, and that he was hugging me. You could see by the expression on his face, and the way he was hugging me, that this man loved me. I was still sceptical at this point, but then what you said next took any scepticism I had away forever! You told me he was taking a comb from his back pocket and combing his hair from one side to the next, and forming a small quiff at the front. And that when he smiled he had no back teeth. You described my late father so well I knew he was there with us. You went on to explain how he visited me often, how he felt at his time of passing, and so much more. I left you that day, 6 years after my dad's passing, feeling so full of love. You made me feel and realise that he is always going to be somewhere, and that the end really isn't the end. I *finally had acceptance. After not even being able to talk about my dad, I went to knowing that one day I will see him again.*

A few nights later, I had the most realistic dream I have ever experienced. My dad visited me, and I hugged him and sat with him while he told me that everything would be ok. When I awoke from that dream, I was, and still am, convinced that I actually hugged my dad that night. I remember the feel of his jumper and the smell of him, so well.

I honestly believe that your reading that day was meant to be, and it took me off a bad path and directed me to a better one, and for that I thank you."

****

A Being Of Light

This is a little bit of something I remembered only last night. It occurred when my youngest daughter, who is now twenty seven, was aged around four years old. I wasn't in the house that day, but it was witnessed by the rest of the family - who were all utterly convinced, I have to say.

We were renting a one-storey house, situated amongst fields, in the middle of nowhere. The bathroom, which was an old converted animal shelter, had been built onto the living room. The children and their father were watching television - when Lauren's attention was very suddenly caught - by something that she says glided across the room, before disappearing into the bathroom (through the closed door!). I don't think that the rest of the family actually saw it themselves, but they all testified that her head whipped around at great speed, and her eyes were like saucers! When I returned home, the incident was animatedly relayed, and I asked Lauren to draw a picture of what she had seen... and she produced what I can only describe as a gingerbread man shaped image - which, she explained, glowed brightly. Apparently, it didn't pay attention to anyone in the room, but simply moved across the floor, in the direction of the bathroom, and vanished (maybe it was desperate for the loo!). I really couldn't imagine what our visitor could be. An alien, maybe? I have never, in my entire life, seen anything that resembled what she described, but I absolutely believed her. It could even have been the vibrant energy field of a non-physical being, rather than the being itself (which might not have been visible). Anyway, the most important thing is that it didn't leave behind any kind of negative or unsettling residue. And, to my knowledge, it was never seen again. Which doesn't mean, of course, that it, or others, weren't still around... or maybe even just continuing to pass through!

Final word

Well, that was a bit of a foray into the mind and opinions of just one largely unimportant (in the grand scheme of things) mostly-retired medium! Having said that, every life *is* very important in its own way. We don't all start on a level playing field, that's for sure; some begin with an obvious advantage, others with a very clear *dis*advantage. There is much about the world that I don't understand and struggle to come to terms with. I won't be here in another 50 years for sure, but all of that stuff probably will be - and maybe the yet-to-come souls will be able to offer valuable insights that are currently eluding us. Of course, those souls will only be able to build upon the foundation created by *us*, the leaving souls, and I hope that I will have contributed something of worth, even if it is only in the eyes of a handful of people. Whenever I feel overwhelmed and hopeless, I try to remember that, although I cannot change and heal the entire world, I *can* positively add to the *collective* energy, in my own individual way.

After all, let us not forget what the little old lady said, as she peed in the sea: "every little helps!"

I wish for you all to experience productive lives filled with love and creativity, worthwhile challenges, and a myriad of *aha* moments! And finally, whilst we're on the subject of yet-to-come souls, I thought that this might be the ideal time to blow the dust off a poem I wrote many moons ago; somehow, given the current social climate, it feels particularly relevant:

Bless The Newborn Child

A brand new day, a golden dawn,

Pure magic when a child is born.

A baby's breath, the sweetest air,

Gives rise to joy the world should share,

And softest skin of angel down

Is red or yellow, white or brown -

A rainbow bright of every hue,

The gift of life for me and you.

Tomorrow's folk yet still to grow,

In far off lands of sun or snow,

All babies equal in their worth -

The newborn keepers of our Earth.

To north and south, to east and west,

May every child be loved and blessed.

Bonus pages (Chapters 1 and 2):

How The 'Dead' Connect With Us...
And Vice Versa

Chapter 1

See, feel, hear.

Many years ago, when I used to travel out to conduct my work, there was an occasion on which the lady of the house led me up a steep set of stairs to a converted loft. There was a small table and chairs set up, and the idea was that her guests - my customers - would join me, one at a time, to receive their consultation.

Now, this particular group was in no hurry, and there was a long wait between one customer descending the stairs and the next ascending; I was becoming a tad impatient, thinking, "I am going to be here all night if this carries on!" Suddenly, I became aware of a tingling pressure on my top lip, and the face of a little girl very close to my own - she had just kissed me! I clearly heard the words, "can she *see* me?" and the child, holding onto the hand of an adult who was out of my vision, was gently led backward; as she realised that yes, I *could* see her, she smiled delightedly and waved. She appeared to be around six years old with dark, wavy hair tumbling to her shoulders, and the sweetest smile. I gave a little wave in return, and she faded away. I never discovered the identity of my lovely little visitor, but what really struck me was her excitement and wonder when she realised that I could see her, as if that was an oddity, an unusual occurrence. As if I was the 'ghost' in *her* world.

Something else happened, too, whilst I was cooling my heels in that loft; a man and woman silently climbed the stairs and sat on chairs (that were not actually there) placed in front of the wall opposite to where I was sitting. They appeared, for all the world, to be waiting for an appointment; they didn't acknowledge me and not a word passed between them. Minutes ticked by with no sign of my next customer, and I watched as the couple stood up and headed back down the stairs. "That was bloody odd!" I mused. Anyway, the awaited lady finally arrived… and the silent visitors returned, settling themselves down. I described them to her, and she was immediately emotional: "That's my mother and father!" she whispered. For the life of me, I cannot remember what was communicated that day, but I am happy to report that they didn't remain silent and that their daughter was really happy to hear from them.

There are many ways in which *we* connect with non-physical dimensions, and they with us. I believe that some form of communication is always at play, whether or not we are aware. I myself have developed the ability to see (known as clairvoyance) and to feel (known as clairsentience). I don't 'see' beings with my eyes as such; it is more like seeing with my mind... and not in solid form, as if they are here, in the physical world; they appear more like holograms, which makes some sense to me. This snippet from Wikipedia explains it well:

"Typically, a **hologram** is a photographic recording of a light field, rather than an image formed by a device without a lens."

Deceased people and spiritual entities don't have a physical body in the way that we do, and so they are creating and presenting an *energetic* image of themselves, as a way of connecting with us and producing 'evidence'. We operate in a dimension in which we recognise and make sense of things through the conscious senses, and any being that wishes to communicate with us has to be able to do so in a language that we recognise and understand (and vice versa, of course). I have heard mediums say that they see those they are communicating with as if they are as solid as you and me, and that might well be true for them... it just isn't for me. Having said that, I do remember suddenly waking one night to see a man standing beside the bed, level with my head - and he *did* appear to be solid. Even though I was bleary-eyed, I could see that he sported a thick beard and scruffy, dark hair, was wearing a blue, round-neck tee shirt, and trousers that were baggy at the knees - and, even though I couldn't see them, I knew for sure that he was wearing tatty grey socks and no shoes. He was staring at *me*, too, and I swear that that is what woke me up! However, within seconds he disappeared and I still can't say for sure whether he was just a figment of my imagination or an actual non-physical entity. I had no idea who he was and still don't... but I picked up on a strong sense of irritability and grumpiness!

However, seeing is only one aspect of how it all works for me; *feeling* is the most important part of the process. And, when I say feeling, I don't just mean happy, sad, hot, cold etc. I wish I could explain it more clearly (and I *have* tried to do so many times): there is a knowingness that comes through feeling, an instant understanding that emanates from within my mind. If I were to describe it in physical terms, I would say that it is kind of like a liquid that drips into the centre of my head and then spreads out. I find the feeling more informative and interesting than the seeing; the seeing without the feeling would be akin to gazing upon lifeless, cardboard cutouts, and I wouldn't enjoy that. I like to experience the essence of the communicator, to feel how they feel, and to understand who they were/are as a soul.

However, in the world of mediumship, the way in which I work isn't always what the customer is hoping for, and I have no problem being upfront about this. I do not consider myself to be the greatest medium on the planet, although I have had some satisfying results and a respectable number of happy customers. I am unable to say things like, "I have a connection with your Uncle Bob here; he was 63 years old when he passed, and he lived at number 23 Park Grove, and he loved Manchester United football team." I remember one Scottish medium claiming in the press that unless a reader can come up with names and other such specific details, then they aren't the real deal. Well, many would agree with him, but you can only be open to communication in the way that you are able to receive it… and, often, it is the seemingly most insignificant detail that can be the most meaningful to a grieving customer. I always gave the best I could, over a period of 25 years - and, I say *gave* because I no longer do much in the way of mediumship these days - but it never felt enough to me. I always wanted to be able to see, feel, and provide *more*!

What I *could* and did do with the skills I developed was to physically describe the soul with whom I was connecting, and express what I was feeling about them - their personality, their way of looking at life, and how they were, just prior to their passing. And, of course, I would explain all that was communicated to me in terms of 'messages'. I didn't tend to automatically know who they were, as in mother, father etc; I would simply pass on all of the information that I was able to receive and decipher, and the customer would usually have no difficulty in recognising the communicator. However, I came to the conclusion that it made more sense to be able to 'tune in' directly, and so I started to ask, "who is it, specifically, that are you hoping to make a connection with today?" This enabled me to make what I jokingly referred to as a 'cosmic phone call'... and it proved to be very effective! I would send out my thoughts to the requested loved one, and, more often than not, a connection was made... and usually *other* connections, too. Some people see this as 'cheating', believing that it is the medium's job to be able to know exactly who they wish to make a link with *and* provide the consultation; after 20 plus years, I had no interest in being 'tested' before I could get on with my work. I was always more invested in the results than in how many marks out of ten I might be awarded! I am aware that many mediums say that they have no control over who 'comes through', and that 'spirit' chooses. Again, for them, I am sure that that is true; it just isn't the way that I see it, or how I work. No-one is right, and no-one is wrong; it just comes down to personal style and preference. And, in case anyone wonders, I would only ask for the relationship of the deceased to the customer, *or* the first name and age at the time of passing. I didn't go looking things up, and even if I did try, it wouldn't have been effective because it wouldn't have provided me with the kind of information I was interested in.

So far, I have been talking about myself and how I learned to connect with non-physical souls. But, what about you? The wonderful thing about clairsentience is that we all possess the skill, whether or not we recognise it. We all feel our way through life; we all sense things; we all sometimes just *know* something without understanding *how* we know it. You might not be working as a professional medium, but that doesn't mean that you aren't clairsentient - you are! However, you may also find - with a little experimenting - that you are also clairvoyant and have a strong ability to 'see' with your mind, or you might discover that you are clairaudient, and able to 'hear'. The late, much-loved Doris Stokes delivered most of her work clairaudiently, which worked extremely well for her and those with whom she worked.

The chances are high that you will have strongly sensed the presence of someone who isn't physically there; you will have 'picked up' certain feelings from others around you, maybe without even realising; you will have found that a particular person suddenly entered your mind and stayed there, for no obvious reason; you will have been aware of the 'energetic sense' of an unfamiliar room or building you ventured into, in either a pleasant way or an uncomfortable way. This is *you* knowing stuff through feeling, and it is the same ability that is used by mediums. It isn't a gift that only a select few possess: it is something that *everyone* has been endowed with - a skill that can definitely be developed and strengthened.

Chapter 2

Weird… but completely true!

I was going to explain to you how I started to develop my ability to intuitively see and feel, thinking that it might be helpful to you… and then I remembered something that I haven't thought about for quite some time - something that is probably going to sound weird, not to mention entirely invented by a disturbed mind! However, I promise you that what I am going to tell you is absolutely true, *and* relevant to the title of this book.

I started to consciously work on energetic development around 1990, but toward the mid 90's I took it more seriously (eventually leading me to abandon my career in advertising sales to become a full-time intuitive consultant). In the meantime, I organised a little office in the corner of my bedroom, which became the setting for my strange story.

I had read a book about automatic writing and decided to give it a try. I would sit with an open notepad, pen poised as if to write… and wait. It didn't take very long for the pen to start writing, with me doing nothing more than holding it loosely, ballpoint resting lightly on the paper. At first, it was nothing more than scribble, but I persevered - and actual words and sentences started to appear. I came up with questions to ask, and answers that were not consciously known to me were supplied. At the time, I had developed an idea for a magazine for teens and was working on the editorial content, as well as drumming up advertising revenue. Through this, I came to know a young man and woman who were involved in youth work, and I would sometimes visit their office for a cup of tea and a catch-up. I told them all about my little hobby, and they were fascinated: "do it for us!" they begged… and so I did. I sat with my pad and pen and invited them to ask questions to which I couldn't possibly know the answer. I won't go into detail, but suffice to say my new friends were utterly blown away. In fact, they were shocked, and so was I. Where *was* this information coming from??

Increasingly, it felt to me that I was dealing with an actual communicator, and so I asked for their name - which was duly supplied via the automatic writing. I now have no memory of that name but *do* remember that it sounded 'foreign' to me, a name I was unfamiliar with. Even my friends started to talk about 'him' as if they knew him: "what does ***** have to say, today? Can I ask him a question?"

But then, there came about a new and strange development. I received a written message from someone who claimed to be called Connor Ross, a young man who had lived in East Kilbride, Scotland, and who had passed as a result of cancer. He told me that he wanted to get in touch with his widow, Louise, who was staying with his father... and he gave me the address. I rang directory enquiries, expecting them to say that they had nothing listed; instead, they informed me that the name of the person at that address was actually Rossi, not Ross - and that it was an ex-directory (unlisted) telephone number. They were not allowed to give it out.

I was gobsmacked. Okay, the name was slightly different... but the man actually existed... and the address was correct! I returned to my pad and explained the situation - and was given the name and address of a neighbour to contact. Once again I called directory enquiries, and once again there was one slight inaccuracy: the lady in question *did* exist, but the number of her house was different. They gave me her phone number, and I called, explaining that I was trying to get in touch with Mr Rossi, and was hoping that she would be kind enough to take *my* number and pop it through his door. I can't remember how I explained having *her* details, but she was a lovely lady, and did as I asked.

When Mr Rossi called me, my face was as red as a stop-light, and my hands were shaking; he was going to think I was head-case... a stalker, even. Stammering and stuttering, I asked if he was the father of Connor, who had sadly passed from cancer and was the late husband of Louise. He immediately and emphatically said *no...* he did not have a deceased son and had never heard of Connor Rossi. Embarrassed and deflated, I quickly apologised, before ringing off. Luckily, he didn't ask me why I wanted to know this stuff, so I didn't have to explain that some invisible entity had sent me on a wild goose chase! But still, there was so much that was correct. I have never, ever been to East Kilbride, and had never heard the name Connor Rossi until that time. It was highly unnerving... and yet massively impressive, at the same time!

However, that wasn't quite the end of it all. I chewed it over and eventually went back to my pad in the early hours of the morning, writing about what had happened, and demanding an explanation. Once again my pen took on a life of its own, and a telephone number appeared on the page. Maybe this was where I was going to find the answer, but I certainly couldn't call *anyone* in the wee small hours. I went back to bed and tried to sleep; as soon as it was an acceptable time to make a phone call, I dialled that number - and *this* is what I heard:

"Hello, Scottish Widows Life Insurance And Pensions, can I help you?"

I slammed the phone down and knew for sure that I had been played like a fiddle! A Scottish guy looking for his widowed wife? The *Scottish Widows* Company? What a hilarious joke - I *don't* think! I realised that I had unwittingly become the plaything of... well, I don't know *what* it was. I was exhausted and vowed never again to communicate with my tormentor. It didn't give up easily, though. For days after, my hand would periodically buzz and vibrate, and I just knew that it was trying to get me to communicate again. However, I had finally had enough, and set out to learn how to use my intuitive ability in a safer, more sustainable way. Despite the craziness, I know that I will always retain a sense of eerie wonderment that such an experience was even possible! I can't say for sure whether it was a 'dark' entity trying to gain control of my mind, or just a very mischievous soul who was having a giggle at my naive expense. Either way, I

149

wasn't willing to hang around to find out! You can see why this genuinely truthful story deserves to be included in a book about the ways in which we can connect with the 'dead' - and the ways in which *they* can connect with *us*!

Contacting Leanne Halyburton online:

www.leannehalyburton.com

spiritoflife@hotmail.co.uk

https://www.facebook.com/StoriesByLeanne

Printed in Great Britain
by Amazon

58072845R00090